AT THE TOMB

CHARLES LUDWIG

WARNER PRESS, INC.
Anderson, Indiana

Published by
Warner Press, Inc.
Anderson, Indiana

All scripture passages, unless otherwise indicated, are from the King James Version ©1972 by Thomas Nelson or the Revised Standard Version ©1972 by Thomas Nelson, or The Holy Bible, New International Version. Copyright ©1973, 1978, 1984 International Bible Society. Used by permission of Zondervan Bible Publishers.

Copyright © 1991 by Warner Press, Inc.
ISBN 0-87162-514-8   Stock #D8150
All Rights Reserved
Printed in the United States of America
Warner Press, Inc.

Arlo F. Newell, Editor in Chief
Dan Harman, Book Editor
Cover by David Liverett

Other books from Warner Press by Charles Ludwig:
  Wonderful Jesus (1942)
  The Adventures of Juma (1944)
  Witch Doctor's Holiday (1945)
  Christ at the Door (1946)
  Leopard Glue (1946)
  Sankey Still Sings (1947)
  Cannibal Country (1948)
  Momma Was a Missionary (1963)
  On Target (1963)
  Spinning Shoes (1988)
  At the Cross (1989)

Dedication

For my daughter Brenda whose main goal in life is helping others.

Table of Contents

Foreword vii

Chapter

  1. Was Jesus Really Dead? 1

     Map of Jerusalem during
     the ministry of Jesus 7

  2. Did Jesus Really Die on the Cross 15

  3. A Rich Man's Tomb 27

  4. A Day in Old Jerusalem 37

  5. Friday Evening 47

  6. Passover 57

  7. The Longest Night 69

  8. Easter Morning 85

  9. Those World-Changing Appearances 99

10. They Met the Resurrected Christ 108

11. Did Jesus Really Rise From the Dead? 119

12. The Empty Tomb 131

13. The Meaning of the Empty Tomb 141

Answers to the Questions 151

For Further Reading 162

Footnotes 162

Selected Bibliography 163

Works Cited 164

Foreword

During the period in which Jesus Christ lived, that is from the time of the Herods to the destruction of Jerusalem, there were four high priests named Jesus: Jesus, son of Fabus; Jesus, son of Sic; Jesus, son of Damneus; and Jesus, son of Gamiliel (Josephus).

Except for technical scholars, those high priests named Jesus are forgotten. But Jesus of Nazareth, *our* high priest (Hebrews 10:21), who was crucified to pay the penalty of *our* sins, is still remembered by the masses. Why?

Because only Jesus of Nazareth was resurrected from the dead!

* * *

Just as the invention of the digit zero revolutionized mathmatics, the fact of the Empty Tomb can revolutionize the lives of believers.

Faith in his empty tomb is the key to unlimited creativity, joy—and satisfaction. The resurrection of Jesus Christ has mind-boggling implications. Overwhelmed by Beethoven, George Santayana exclaimed: "God made the world and the universe in order that Beethoven might compose the Ninth!" That is gross exaggeration. But a far more overwhelming fact is not an exaggeration. That fact is this: *God allowed his only begotten Son to be crucified, and then raised him from the dead in order that our lives might count!*

Faith in the cross and empty tomb dries tears . . . assures immortality . . . provides motivation . . . straightens shoulders . . . cancels sin . . . mends broken hearts.

Faith in the cross, the empty tomb, and the atonement is, of course, necessary just to be a Christian. Paul is emphatic: "But if there is no resurrection of the dead, then Christ has not been risen; if Christ has not been raised, then our preaching is in vain, and your faith is in vain" (1 Cor. 15:13-14, NIV).

In his *Church Dogmatics*, Karl Barth bore down heavily on this fact: "We may be Protestants or Catholics, Lutherans or Reformed, to the right or the left, but in some way, we must have seen and heard the angels at the open and empty tomb if we are to be sure of our ground."

Across the centuries, this has proven to be true. Whenever we study the lives of God's giants: William Carey, Brother Lawrence, David Livingstone, Mother Teresa, Telemachus, Charles Tinley, and others, we come face to face with one similarity: *All of God's giants have had an intense personal faith in the crucifixion, and resurrection of Jesus Christ!*

Satan loathes the Empty Tomb; and to keep us from having access to its power, he uses devious arguments. Mouthing such words as hallucination, mass hysteria, and unreliable legends, he persuades many who pride themselves on being sophisticated, to dismiss the New Testament as a document filled with idle tales.

Like other skeptics, Sigmund Freud considered the doctrine of the resurrection to be merely a mental projection. Nonetheless it is not difficult to ignore these worldly "wise" ones when we remember that such doubters have often been proven to be dead wrong.

Scientists assured the world that humans could never fly; that to change magnetism into electricity was impossible; that humankind could never visit the moon—

and that the sun moved around the earth. But they were proven wrong by numerous Christians who believed implicitly in the empty tomb:

Wilbur and Orville Wright, sons of a bishop, flew.

Copernicus, a lay priest, risked his life by publishing the fact that the earth revolves around the sun.

Michael Faraday, a dedicated Christian and occasional preacher, discovered how to convert magnetism into electricity.

John Dalton, a devout Quaker, developed the Atomic Theory.

And by discovering and publishing some of God's laws, Isaac Newton provided a way to get to the moon and back.

Indeed, basic technology is balanced on the shoulders of those who accepted the facts proclaimed by the Empty Tomb.

Ah, but could those brilliant scientists have been mistaken?

* * *

Frankly, there are problems connected to Jesus' resurrection, especially for those who have never experienced the new birth, and thus have never felt the living presence of Christ. Moreover, many of these problems begin with the New Testament account.

One problem concerns dates. If the resurrection is really true, why did the Gospel writers wait so long to document it? That's a good question, for Mark, probably the first Gospel to be written, was not completed until around A.D. 55 at the earliest, and the other Gospels did not appear until from twenty to forty years later.

Another difficulty concerns the hour during which Jesus was nailed to the cross. According to Mark, and his schedule agrees with Matthew and Luke, "it was the third hour" (15:25). But John wrote that Jesus was standing before Pilate at "about the sixth hour" (19:14). This means that three hours after the time of crucifixion attested to by Matthew, Mark, and Luke, Jesus was still in the midst of his trial!

Here's another. Who was first to see the resurrected Christ? Matthew tells us: "As they [Mary Magdalene and the other Mary (v.1)] went to tell his disciples, behold Jesus met them, saying All hail, and they came and held him by the feet, and worshipped him" (28:9).

But Mark's record is slightly different: "Now when Jesus was risen early the first day of the week, he appeared *first* to Mary Magdalene, out of whom he had cast seven devils" (16:9, emphasis added).

But according to Luke, it seems that he first appeared to Peter, "[Those who met him on the way to Emmaus] rose that same hour and returned to Jerusalem; and they found the eleven gathered together and them that were with them, who said, The Lord has risen indeed, and has appeared to Simon!" (24:33-34). Paul's version agreed with that of Luke: "He appeared to Cephas [Peter], then of the twelve" (1 Cor. 15:5).

But what did John have to say? "Saying this she [Mary Magdalene] turned round and saw Jesus standing, but she did not know that it was Jesus" (20:14).

Such problems are merely the beginning!

One purpose of this book is to examine the most obvious difficulties and to do so in a way that can be understood. Like *At the Cross* (Ludwig 1989) it is divided into thirteen chapters accompanied by questions and answers. Thus, it is an ideal quarterly study-book.

1 Was Jesus Really Dead?

Satan hates the empty tomb with passion—and he has a sound reason to hate it; for the empty tomb is the culmination of a series of defeats that cancelled his power over believers.

From the beginning of Jesus' ministry, Satan faced violent disappointments. One of the sorest of these developed immediately after Jesus commissioned the Seventy. On that occasion, Satan's imps—even the most experienced imps—suddenly found themselves helpless and frustrated before each worker whom Jesus had commissioned to spread the Good News.

Satan was intensely concerned, and as the weeks and months passed, his concern deepened; for, almost every day, he witnessed sights that gouged at his eyes. It was with sublime horror that he watched Jesus raise Lazarus from the dead, heal the sick, feed the multitude—and show followers how to resist Satan.

Then on Easter morning he was astounded to see

Jesus rise from the dead and step out of the empty tomb.

Reasoning from experience, Satan must have squirmed when he considered the power of this fact, for the empty tomb underlined the accuracy of every statement of Jesus including these:

I will never leave thee, nor forsake thee. . . . (Heb. 13:5).

He that believeth on me, the works that I do shall he do also, and greater works than these shall he do; because I go unto my Father. (John 14:12).

Where two or three are gathered in my name, there am I in the midst of them. (Matt. 18:20).

* * *

To Satan, those promises—accented by the empty tomb—are far worse than acid in the eyes, and to neutralize them, he has dedicated his talents to convince the world that the fact of the resurrection is nothing but a myth. One can almost see and hear him speaking to a conference of imps, "We must not allow the fact of the resurrection to be believed. Here is the strategy that you will follow:

1. Convince the world that when Jesus was placed in the tomb he was not actually dead, but was merely unconscious; and that the cool tomb was so invigorating that he acquired sufficient strength to escape both the shroud and the imprisoning tomb.

2. If that does not convince them, persuade them that the body in the tomb was that of another who was still alive." A variation of this argument is advanced in the Koran (*Quar'an*).

The most popular and plausible of these Satanic arguments is that Jesus was not actually dead, and so we'll focus on that contention. Let's begin by admitting that at the time of his death, Jesus had only been on the cross for six hours. Mark tells us that Pilate "marvelled" when he heard that Jesus was dead. Why did he marvel? Because frequently those who had been crucified lingered for days before death released them from their agony. Also, live people have been buried by mistake. Such an incident almost happened during World War 1.

In the midst of a battle, a would-be rescuer carefully inched his way across no-man's-land in order to rescue Captain Bernard L. Montgomery. But just as he reached him, the friendly helper was killed. Later, after the German retreat, Montgomery was placed on a stretcher and rushed to the hospital. An examination indicated that shrapnel had entered both lungs. Agreeing that he was dead, his grave was dug. But as the attendant who accompanied the body to the grave watched, he noticed one of the captain's eyes had flickered.

The driver sped to the hospital. The "dead" man recovered. He is now remembered as Field Marshall Sir Bernard L. Montgomery.

Monty saved North Africa for the Allies.

Could a similar mistake have happened to Jesus?

Since the facts are clear, we will scrutinize them. According to Mark, Jesus was nailed to the cross at the *third* hour—that is 9 A.M. (15:25). Mark also indicates that Jesus died six hours later during the *ninth* hour—3 P.M. (v. 33).

Neither Matthew nor Luke mention the hour when the nails were hammered through his wrists (Ludwig, 1989, 65). But by simple mathematics we know that all three agreed as to the time of his crucifixion. This is obvious because each states the time of the great darkness that enveloped the earth—and also the time of his death. See Matthew 27:45-46; Mark 15:33-37; and Luke 23:44-46.

John alone disagrees (19:6). But there is an explanation. Gleason Archer states: "John was following the official numbering system of the Roman civil day. The evidence for a civil day that began numbering the hours after midnight is quite decisive. Pliny the Elder (*Natural History* 2:77) makes the following observation: 'The day itself has been differently observed in different countries: by the Babylonians between two sunrises; by the Athenians between two sunsets; by the Umbrians from noon to noon; by the Roman priests from midnight to midnight' " (Archer 1982). The Jews measured time from sunrise to sunset. "Are there not twelve hours in a day?" (John 11:9).

But why would John use a different time system than the others? Because he wrote the Fourth Gospel in Ephesus!

Thus, there can be no doubt that Jesus was nailed between the two thieves at approximately 9 A.M. (Incidentally, there is a simple way to figure Bible time. All one has to do is to go straight across the clock from the hour hand. Crossing from 3 we get 9; and going up from 6 we get 12.)

There is no record that either of the thieves had been scourged, mocked, or taken from one tribunal to another as had Jesus. All three of the synoptic writers mention that the cross was placed on the shoulders of Simon of Cyrene. Matthew and Mark say that he was "compelled" to carry it, while Luke merely said, "And as they led him away, they laid hold upon one Simon, a Cyrenian, coming out of the country, and on him they laid the cross, that he might bear it after Jesus" (23:26). Curiously, the Simon of Cyrene detail was not mentioned by John.

This episode indicates that Jesus was already half

dead even before the first spike was driven. But to really grasp the reality of his utter exhaustion we must review what he endured between the Last Supper and his crucifixion.

In doing this, a helpful step is to follow his path on the map on page 7.

Moreover, as we follow his steps, we must keep in mind that after his final supper with the disciples, he had not had anything to eat or drink until a sponge filled with vinegar was pushed up to his lips while he was suspended by the nails on the cross (Matt. 27:48; Mark 15:36; Luke 23:36; John 19:29).

That Thursday night, following a series of lessons and challenges—John 13-17—Jesus led the disciples across the Kidron Valley to the Garden of Gethsemane, a little over a mile away. It was Passover week, the moon was full, and so their route was clear. Even so, being emotionally exhausted—he had washed the disciples' feet, and Judas had already left to betray him—Jesus lacked the necessary strength to hurry.

Moreover, each step meant that he was that much closer to the most heartrending decision of his life.

Before entering the garden he said to his disciples "Sit ye here, while I shall pray" (Mark 14:32). See also Matthew 26:36.

Next, he "took with him Peter and the two sons of Zebedee, and began to be sorrowful and very heavy. Then saith he unto them, My soul is exceeding sorrowful, even unto death: tarry ye here, and watch with me. And he went a little farther, and fell on his face, and prayed, saying, O my Father, if it be possible, let this cup pass from me: nevertheless not as I will, but as thou wilt" (Matt. 26:37-39).

This was a strength-draining occasion, and Dr. Luke intensified the terrible scene as recorded by Matthew and Mark (14:33-42) by adding the fact: "There appeared an angel unto him from heaven, strengthening him. And being in an agony he prayed more earnestly: and his sweat was as it were great drops of blood falling down to the ground" (Luke 22:43-44).

Wrestling with his will consumed energy, for it meant agreeing to drain that terrible cup—a cup that reeked with the vilest of stenches, and was putrid with the sins of the world from the beginning of time until the end.

It was like draining blood from the jugular.

In addition, having to awaken Peter, James, and John on the three occasions when they fell asleep, consumed even more energy.

* * *

After he had spiritually prepared for death on the cross, Jesus was arrested. See Matthew 26:50; Mark 14:46; Luke 22:54; and John 18:12. From this point on, as we follow his steps, we must keep in mind that each step and each incident was an overwhelming, energy-consuming burden.

Following his arrest, Jesus was led to the home of Annas. Here we have a problem, for John wrote that they "led him away to *Annas* first" (18:13).

But Matthew said: "They that laid hold on Jesus led him away to *Caiaphas* the high priest" (26:57). Mark did not use the name Caiaphas. Rather he said, "They led Jesus away to the high priest" (14:53). Luke, in turn, stated, "Then they took him, and led him, and brought him into the high priest's house" (22:54).

What is the solution? Was Matthew mistaken? The answer is that Annas had been the high priest, that five of his sons had been high priests, and that Caiaphas, the current high priest, was his son-in-law. Also, according to Jewish tradition, Annas was still honored as the high priest. Luke adds force to this by his statement in Acts: "Annas the high priest, and Caiaphas, and John, and

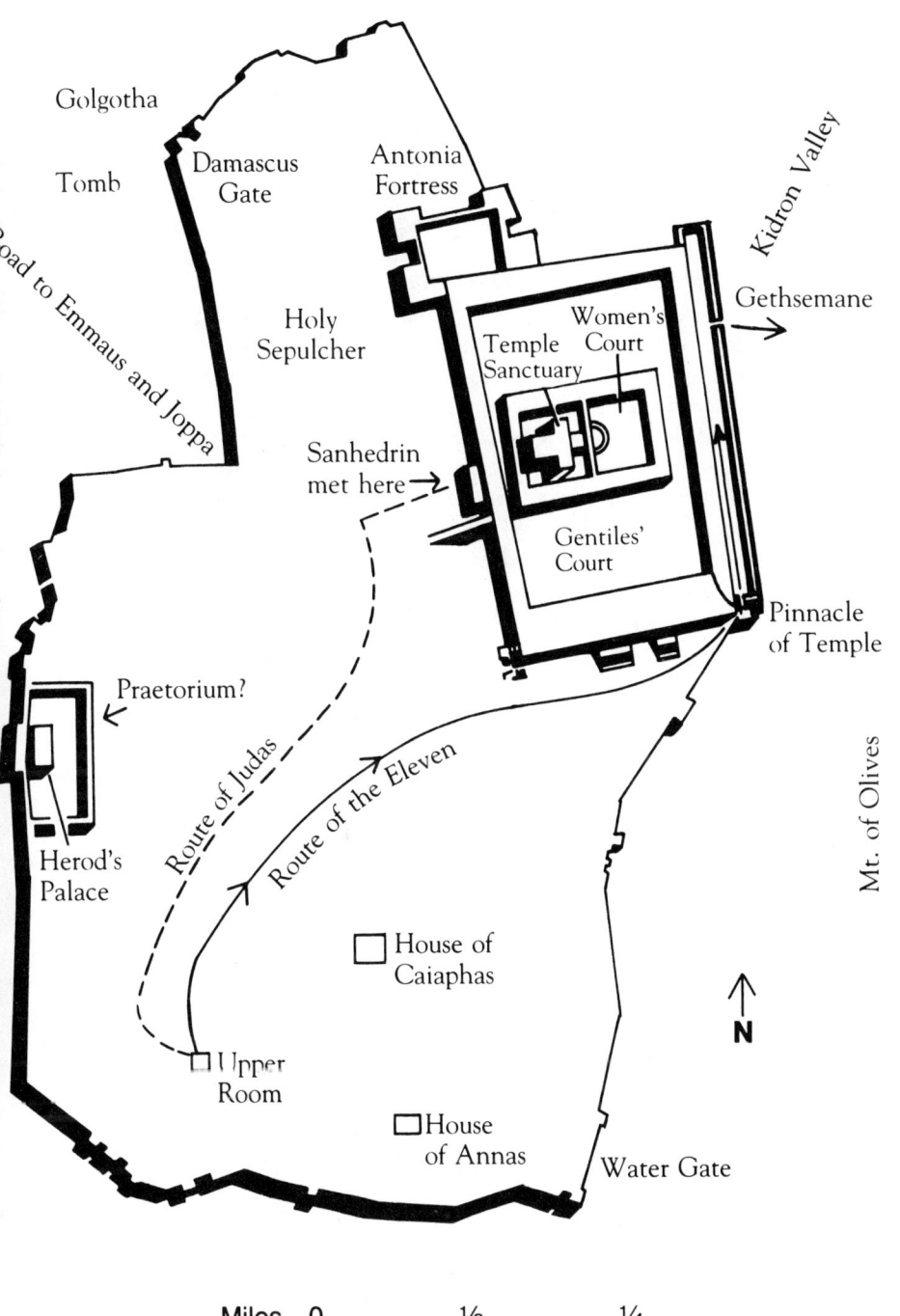

Alexander, and as many as were of the kindred of the high priest, were gathered at Jerusalem" (4:6).

The official reason why Jesus was taken to Annas is unknown. Perhaps this incidental maneuver was to delay the proceedings so that Caiaphas would have time to assemble a quorum. A quorum of twenty-three members of the Sanhedrin was required in order that any session would be legal. Also, by glancing at the map, we can see that the home of the wealthy and tottering Annas was on the way to the palace of Caiaphas less than a quarter of a mile to the northwest.

As Jesus was led from the home of Annas to the palace of Caiaphas he passed the Upper Room. It was slightly to his left. As he did so, his mind may have flooded with painful and recent memories—memories that dipped into his already low reserve of energy.

Additional heartache awaited in the palace of Caiaphas. Combining gospel accounts, we learn that while there he was slapped, spat upon, mocked, blindfolded, and punched around. Likewise, Jesus suffered knowing that as Peter was warming his hands in the courtyard, he not only denied him three times, but also colored his denials with disgraceful, fishermen's oaths.

As Jesus waited before the Sanhedrin, Caiaphas—in spite of the jewels of office that winked on his chest—was a frustrated man. Being a Sadducee, he had no hope of future life; and he felt humiliated for the masses to consider his father-in-law the *real* high priest. In addition, he feared Herod. In a moment of passion, Herod had ordered that the head of John the Baptist be brought into the banquet hall on a platter; furthermore, his father, Herod the Great, had drowned a high priest even though he was his brother-in-law! But at the moment he had another frustration. He just could not get a reliable person to testify against Jesus (Matt. 26:59-60, and Mark 14:55).

Finally, however, Matthew noted:
> At the last came two false witnesses, And said, "This fellow said, 'I am able to destroy the temple of God, and rebuild it in three days' " (26:60-61).

That statement brightened the eyes of Caiaphas, even though Mark included the detail: "But neither so did their witness agree together" (14:59).

Encouraged, Caiaphas asked, "Art thou the Christ, the Son of the Blessed?" (Mark 14:61). Then, while stroking his beard as he awaited an answer, Jesus, who had been silent, replied: "I am: and ye shall see the Son of man sitting on the right hand of power, and coming in the clouds of heaven" (v. 62).

At this point Caiaphas "rent his clothes." Then in the manner of a cat shaking a mouse, he exclaimed, "What need we any further witnesses? Ye have heard the blasphemy: what think ye?" (vv. 63-64).

The eager Sanhedrin answered at once. "They all condemned him to be guilty of death" (v. 64).

Later, perhaps around 7 A.M., Jesus was led from the palace of Caiaphas to the Praetorium—Pilate's judgment hall. (The exact location of this Gentile building is obscure. Some researchers place it near the Antonia Fortress and others at the magnificent palace built by Herod the Great. If it was near the Herodian Palace on the west side, it was considerably less than a quarter of a mile away; if it was at the Antonia Fortress on the northeast side, it was more than half a mile away.)

John explained why they took him to Pilate. Answering the procurator's statement that they should judge him themselves, the "Jews . . . said unto him. It is not lawful for us to put any man to death" (18:31).

What immediately followed is so familiar we'll not repeat it. Finding a loophole to escape the dilemma that snared him, Pilate pointed out that since Jesus was a

Galilean, he was actually under the jurisdiction of Herod. Next, Luke reported that because Herod had returned to Jerusalem, Pilate decreed that Jesus should be accused before him. (23:6-7).

* * *

After Jesus had refused to defend himself before Herod, "Herod [Antipas] with his men of war set him at nought, and mocked him, and arrayed him in a gorgeous robe, and sent him again to Pilate" (v. 11).
Craving compromise, Pilate decreed that he be chastised.
In obedience to orders, Jesus was fastened to a post and beaten with a whip made of leather thongs, each of which had a bit of chain of metal attached to it.
Lawful Jewish beatings were limited to thirty-nine strokes. But halfway death—the Roman system—had no limitations. The soldiers beat him until they feared that his sagging body might not survive another blow.
His back harrowed with deep slashes, Jesus was returned to Pilate. Again the reluctant Roman tried to avoid the death sentence. This time he gave the mob a choice between Jesus Christ and the notorious criminal—Jesus Barabbas.
The mob chose Barabbas.
Having failed, Pilate succumbed to the shouts of the mob that cried "Crucify him, crucify him" by ceremoniously washing his hands (Matt. 27:24). Then, according to John, Pilate "delivered . . . him therefore unto them to be crucified" (19:16). See also, Mark 15:15 and Luke 23:24.
After having endured tedious hours of trials, beatings, mockery, and Roman halfway death—and after stumbling beneath the weight of the cross made indescribably

heavy by the sins of the world, Jesus finally completed the journey by staggering along the twisting Via Dolorosa—The Way of Sorrows—to "a place called the place of a skull which is called in the Hebrew Golgotha" (John 19:17). There—Luke named it Calvary from the Latin—Jesus was nailed to the cross. The time was 9 A.M. As far as we can determine, the date was Friday, April 7, the 14th of Nisan, A.D. 30. (See appendix for chapter 1.)

As Jesus was hanging on the cross, he continued to endure more pain than that endured by the thieves. The following are some of the reasons for this fact:

He was bearing the sins of the world.

He was utterly exhausted from his series of trials.

His back was raw from the Roman halfway-death.

All of his disciples with the exception of John had forsaken him. Luke, however, indicates that other followers "stood afar off" (23:49).

* * *

Upon his arrival at Golgotha, Jesus was offered a drink designed to modify the pain (Matt. 27:34; Mark 15:23). But determined to bear all the agony crucifixion entailed, Jesus refused it. Nonetheless, no scripture indicates that either of the thieves refused their drinks.

Additional pain was the misery of watching the deepening lines in his mother's face.

At the end of those six harrowing hours, Jesus uttered the most dreadful cry of his life. This is the way Matthew recorded it: "And about the ninth hour Jesus cried with a loud voice, saying, Eli, Eli, lama sabachthani! that is to say, My God, my God, why hast thou forsaken me?" (27:46). Was Jesus merely reciting the first verse of Psalm 22 or did that line express the agony he was enduring?

Evangelicals firmly believe that since Jesus was bearing the sins of the world, he was for a moment, a very brief moment, actually forsaken by God.

Then, after uttering this heartrending cry, Jesus wailed loudly again, " 'It is finished.' With that, he bowed his head, and gave up his spirit" (John 19:30, NIV).

Without contradicting Matthew (27:50) or Mark (15:37), Luke adds the interesting detail that moments before Jesus died, he prayed, "Father, into thy hands I commend my spirit: and having said thus, he gave up the ghost" (23:46).

F. F. Bruce has a comment about his final utterance on the cross. "These words from Psalm 31:5 have for centuries formed part of the evening prayer of pious Jews, and may well have done so for Jesus" (Bruce 1983, 374).

But even though all four Gospels report that Jesus "gave up the ghost," was he *really* dead? Let's examine the facts.

1. The moment Jesus died, "the veil in the temple was rent in twain from the top to the bottom; and the earth did quake, and the rocks rent; and the graves were opened; and many bodies of the saints which slept arose." In response to this "the centurion, and they that were with him, watching Jesus . . . feared greatly, saying, Truly this was the Son of God" (Matt. 27:51-54).

This exclamation of the centurion "and they that were with him" indicates clearly that they believed that Jesus was dead and was indeed "the Son of God." See Mark 15:39 and Luke 23:47.

2. As the ninth hour approached, the Roman soldiers became increasingly nervous; for, the policy of Rome was never to interfere with the religion of anyone under Roman jurisdiction. Jewish law was clear: "If a man have committed a sin worthy of death, and he be to be put to death, and thou hang him on a tree: His body

shall not remain all night upon the tree, but thou shalt in any wise bury him that day; (for he that is hanged is accursed of God)" (Deut. 21:22-23).

Fearing that they would not have time to bury the trio of convicts, two soldiers began to break their legs. This was to make it impossible for them to push themselves up on the cross in order to breathe. "But when they came to Jesus, and saw that he was dead already, they brake not his legs" (John 19:33). One of the soldiers, perhaps to satisfy his curiosity, made certain that Jesus was dead by thrusting a lance into his side. In this way they testified that he was dead. (See John 19:32-34.) Whether the lance was pushed into his left or right side is unknown. But we have the testimony of John "and forthwith there came out blood and water" (19:34). We also have his assurance: "The man who saw it has given testimony, and his testimony is true. He knows that he tells the truth, and he testifies so that you also may believe" (v. 35 NIV).

Pierre Barbet, M.D. commented: "I say wound in the heart and not wound in the side, because this has been attested by tradition, and it has been confirmed by me by experiment. The blow of the lance which was given to the right side reached the right auricle of the heart, perforating the pericardium" (Barbet, n.d., 81).

3. Another testimony that he was dead comes from Mark. We have already quoted him: "Pilate marvelled if he were already dead." Here's the end of that passage: "Calling unto him the centurion, he [Pilate] asked him whether he had been any while dead. And when he knew it of the centurion, he gave the body to Joseph" (15:44-45).

In addition to these major proofs, and there are numerous minor ones, we must mention some of the prophecies that were fulfilled during Jesus' crucifixion. Here are several:

The entire 53rd chapter of Isaiah.
"A bone of him shall not be broken" John 19:36 (Ps. 34:20 and Num. 9:12).
"They shall look on him whom they pierced" John 19:37 (Zech. 12:10).
He would be given vinegar and gall (Ps. 69:21).
Lots would be cast for his garments (Ps. 22:18).

* * *

These proofs are certainly enough to convince any reasonable jury. Still, there is another problem. Was the man on the middle cross with the sign above his head actually Jesus of Nazareth, or was the trick of substitution played on a gullible public?

Our answer to that problem is in the next chapter.

* * *

Can You Answer?

1. At what time was Jesus nailed to the cross?
2. Why did John state an hour that differed from those of the synoptics?
3. How old was Jesus when he died? See appendix.
4. Why didn't the soldiers break Jesus' legs?
5. Name three proofs that Jesus was actually dead.
6. On which side of Jesus' body did the lance enter?
7. How did Pilate know that Jesus was dead?

2 Did Jesus Really Die on a Cross?

Since the cross is a symbol of Christianity, is it absurd to enquire whether or not Jesus of Nazareth actually died on one? Not at all! This is so, for hundreds of millions have been taught that the one who died on that central cross was not the Jesus of the New Testament, but rather that he was an unnamed substitute.

The Koran (*Qur'an*), bible of the Moslem world, is respectful to Jesus. It considers him to have been a major prophet. The Koran even proclaims that he was born of a virgin, that God received him, that he will return—and in Islamic literature, whenever his name is mentioned, it is followed by the words "peace be unto him" or the initials pbuh.

Consider these eloquent lines from the Third Sura (chapter) of the Koran:

"Lord," said Mary, "how shall I have a son seeing no mortal has touched me?" "Even, so,"

God said, "God created what He will. When He decrees a thing He does but say to it 'Be,' and it is."
(Williams n.d., 33.)

* * *

Then, after describing how Jesus became a prophet and how he preached, the Fourth Sura continues:
And they said (in boast),
We killed Christ
Jesus the son of Mary,
The apostle of God:
But they killed him not,
Nor Crucified him,
but it was made
to appear to them so.
(Deedat 1984, 3-4).

Muslims, however, are not the only ones who have questioned whether or not Jesus of Nazareth, the son of Mary, was actually crucified. They, and others, have suggested that the arresting officers could easily have seized the wrong man when they made their arrest in Gethsemane.

In support of this argument, some of the wise ones have asked, "Why was it necessary for Judas to identify Jesus?"

Before answering the statement in the Koran which is as firmly believed by Muslims as is the fact that Jesus was crucified is believed by Christians, we will consider what it would be like if Jesus Christ had never been crucified. Let's think of such a problem on three levels.

* * *

1. If Jesus Christ, God's only begotten Son, had not

fulfilled prophecy by allowing himself to be put to death, countless scriptures in both the Old and New Testaments would be meaningless. The fifty-third chapter of Isaiah, for example, could not be interpreted as referring to Jesus. Moreover, Paul's declaration that "being justified by his blood, we shall be saved from wrath through him" (Romans 5:9), along with John's statement that "the blood of Jesus Christ his Son cleanseth us from all sin" (1 John 1:7) would be as useless as the promises of Satan. Also, dozens of other biblical passages would have little or no meaning.

Indeed, we would have problems with some of the words of Jesus! Had he not been crucified, we would be forced to conclude that he was mistaken when he referred to his forthcoming death.

Those remarks of Jesus are extremely interesting, and it is remarkable how they tended to become more definite as the days drew nearer to his hour of crucifixion. Let's turn to the Gospel according to Matthew and see the way in which the former tax collector quoted him.

"From that time forth began Jesus to show unto his disciples, how that he must go unto Jerusalem, and suffer many things of the elders and chief priests and scribes, and be killed, and be raised again the third day" (16:21).

"And Jesus going up to Jerusalem took the twelve disciples apart in the way, and said unto them, Behold we go up to Jerusalem; and the Son of man shall be betrayed unto the chief priests and unto the scribes, and they shall condemn him to death, and shall deliver him to the Gentiles to mock, and to scourge, and to crucify him and the third day he shall rise again" (20:17-19).

"Ye know that after two days is the feast of the passover, and the Son of man is betrayed to be crucified" (26:2).

These passages prove that Jesus Christ, the Second Person in the Trinity, and the one who said "Before Abraham was, I am" (John 8:58), fully expected to be crucified. He explained this in his own words: "The Son of man came not to be ministered unto, but to minister, and to give his life a ransom for many" (Matt. 20:28).

Had another died in his place, the main thrust of his ministry would have been lost, and all his promises would have been as futile as unsigned checks.

* * *

2. Had Jesus not been crucified as he said he would be, the priceless word *grace* would never have had its New Testament implications. Moreover, the paralyzing result would be that for anyone to request divine forgiveness would be utterly useless.

Intrigued by that five-letter word, Dwight L. Moody read every passage in the Bible where it was mentioned. As he studied the term and its implications he became so excited he rushed downstairs, cornered the first man he met, and demanded that he explain to him the meaning of grace. We do not have a record of what that startled man told Moody, but we do know that grace means God's unmerited favor. It's meaning could be expressed in a simple acrostic: *G*od's *R*edemption *A*t *C*hrist's *E*xpense.

It is through grace that unbelievers, by faith in the atoning work of Christ, are saved.

In his letter to the Ephesians, Paul expressed it this way: "For by grace are ye saved through faith; and that not of yourselves: it is the gift of God: not of works, lest any man should boast" (2:8-9).

Two characteristics of grace that put songs in the hearts of believers are (1) It is limitless. Should every person on earth apply for grace, the supply would not diminish. "But where sin abounded, grace did much more abound" (Romans 5:20). In modern terms, grace is deeper, wider, longer, and higher than outer space; (2) grace is also for *whosoever*. "For God so loved the world that he gave his only begotten Son, that whosoever believeth in him should not perish, but have everlasting life" (John 3:16).

The redeeming power of God's grace was demonstrated after the Nuremberg trials when Pastor Gerecke, the American Protestant pastor assigned to minister to the prisoners, dealt with those in his flock who had been sentenced to hang. Several, including Ribbentrop, confirmed their belief in Christ by celebrating the Lord's Supper with him.

Back in his cell, after hearing his sentence, Ribbentrop nervously paced back and forth while he mumbled, "Death, death. Now I won't be able to write my beautiful memoirs."

When he passed Gerecke as he took his final thirteen steps on the way to the gallows, where the noose with its thirteen knots awaited him, Ribbentrop's farewell was, "I shall see you again." While waiting for the trap to be sprung, he remarked, "Thank God he is merciful." Others made similar statements.

During the trials, several convicts accepted Christ. Some made their confessions to Gerecke, others to Father O'Connor, the American Roman Catholic priest assigned to them.

Did the Lord hear and provide sufficient grace? Certainly! How do we know? For "the blood of Jesus Christ his Son cleanseth from *all* sin" (1 John 1:7)!

On October 15, 1945, while the sounds of buzzing saws and pounding hammers of workmen preparing the scaffolds in the gymnasium drifted into his cell, Ribbentrop indicated his conversion to Christ in a letter that he wrote and addressed to his wife Annelies.

You, my beloved wife, must now devote your stout heart, and all the love which you bestowed on me, to our children. I know I can rely on you. . . . Proud and unbroken, and in the firm belief in an eternal life, I shall go on my way. Farewell—*Auf Wiedersehen* in another world. God be with you.
(Ribbentrop 1953, 201.)

* * *

Fortunately, we know that this forgiving grace can be claimed by anyone: the unfaithful mate, the burglar, the murderer, the blasphemer, or anyone who is aware of *any* sin committed under *any* circumstance.

* * *

3. Had not Jesus been mocked and scourged as we are told in Matthew 27:26; Mark 15:15; Luke 23:8-11; and John 19:1, this planet would indeed be a poorer place on which to live. This is so, for as Isaiah prophesied, "He was wounded for our transgressions, he was bruised for our iniquities; the chastisement of our peace was laid upon him; and with his stripes we are healed" (53:5).

The power of faith in his stripes has been proved to me on many occasions. While living in Kenya with my missionary parents during my teens, I hurt my left ankle while playing soccer. Infection set in, and for two years I was on crutches. Since I was in a rapid-growth period, my left leg became shorter than my right leg. Forced out of school, I was convinced that my life was being wasted. Then I prayed for healing, and during the Christmas season of that year, my wound stopped flowing.

Awakening on Christmas morning I found that I had been healed; and I've never required crutches in the more than fifty years that have followed.

Today my legs are of equal length. The credit belongs to the Lord. Didn't Isaiah prophesy that *by his stripes we are healed?*

I've learned that those words mean far more than physical healing. This fact was brought to my attention at Bergen-Belsen—one of Hitler's most notorious concentration camps.

While visiting this death-trap where tens of thousands perished, my wife Mary and I were guests of a German woman. As we viewed the dismal symbol of people's inhumanity to other human beings, my mind persisted in focusing on Anne Frank, for we had just visited the attic in Amsterdam where she and her family had hidden from the Gestapo.

Bergen-Belsen was the place where she starved to death.

On all sides we saw huge mounds of earth marked with signs: 10,000 LIE HERE; 5,000 LIE HERE; 20,000 LIE HERE. It was heartbreaking. But none of us said a word, for we did not want to embarrass our hostess. Still, memories from *Anne Frank: The Diary of a Young Girl,* kept presenting themselves to me. Each memory emerged like a sharply focused, full-color slide.

Struggling with tears, I saw the fake bookcase which hid the stairs leading up to the secret annex.

Then I saw the ragged family confronted by the Gestapo after the betrayal. (The betrayer was rewarded with seven and a half guilders per Jew; and since the Franks, along with their hidden "guests" numbered eight, his reward totaled sixty guilders.)

It was horrifying. But remembering that we were guests of a considerate German woman, I hesitated to show emotion, but my mind kept returning to Anne.

After her arrest, she was taken to Auschwitz in Poland. A survivor remembered: "I can still see her standing at the door looking down the camp street as a herd of naked gypsy girls was driven by to the crematory, and Anne watched them go and cried. And she cried also when we marched pass the Hungarian children who had already been waiting half a day in the front of the gas chambers because it was not yet their turn. And Anne nudged me and said: 'Look, look. Their eyes . . .' " (Frank 1967, 254).

After that memory it was hard not to reach for my handkerchief. Nonetheless, I managed.

(Due to the approach of the Russians on the Eastern front, Anne, along with others, was moved to Bergen-Belsen. This camp did not have gas chambers; but its streets and buildings were not as clean as those in Auschwitz. Anne found it to be a place of increased suffering.)

Finally, we completed our tour. Near the front we paused at a magnificent shaft that had been erected in honor of those who had perished in the camp.

A fresh wreath had been placed at the base.

As I read the inscription on the shaft, I had to keep biting my lip to maintain control. Then suddenly, out of the corner of my eye, I witnessed a scene that completely overwhelmed me. I saw my German hostess take a sprig of evergreen and with gentle fingers place it on the wreath. That was too much! I broke down. "Do you know the story of Anne Frank," I inquired through my tears.

"Yes," she replied, "I saw it on German television. I was deeply moved—" She hesitated. Then in a slightly husky voice she added, "You see both my husband and my son starved to death in a Russian concentration camp. . . ."

I was speechless. On the way back I began to realize

that woman understood the *Diary of Anne Frank* in much greater depths than I was capable of understanding it. It is thus with Christ! Having been spat upon, crowned with thorns, betrayed, forsaken, beaten—and crucified, he understands. Better yet, he understands, cares—and urgently longs to help. Moreover, he has the necessary power and wisdom to help.

Ah, but what if the Muslims are correct in their claim that "they killed him not, nor crucified him, but it was made to appear to them so?"

If that is true, there is no grace, no forgiveness, no divine understanding of our weaknesses—and no immortality. We, however, must never forget that Paul taught, "For as in Adam all die, even so in Christ shall all be made alive" (1 Cor. 15:22).

The Muslims are wrong—dead wrong! Jesus of Nazareth *was* arrested. Jesus of Nazareth *was* spat upon. Jesus of Nazareth *was* scourged. Jesus of Nazareth *was* nailed to the central cross—and Jesus of Nazareth died on that cross.

Here is evidence:

Judas was given thirty pieces of silver to identify Jesus in Gethsemane. Why? When the Roman garrison stationed at the Antonia fortress was at full strength, it numbered one thousand. Those Roman soldiers paid little attention to the religious rites of the Jews; and, except for a few, they had not met him.

Also, those disciples resembled one another. Many were related. Probably all of them wore beards, had dark eyes—and dressed alike. In fact, it's been reported that James, the son of Alphaeus, could have been mistaken for Jesus.

Considering these possibilities, together with the shadows cast by the olive trees, it is reasonable to suppose that another might have been arrested instead of Jesus.

But in order to understand what happened, we must

go to the Gospel of John and follow the story as he, an eye witness, related it.

As the arresting officers stood before Jesus along with Peter, James, and John, Jesus stepped forward and asked, "Whom seek ye?" (18:4).

After they had answered that they sought Jesus of Nazareth, Jesus said to them, "I am he" (v. 5).

Following that answer, "They went backward, and fell to the ground" (v. 6). "Then [Jesus] asked them again, Whom seek ye? And they said, Jesus of Nazareth. Jesus answered, I have told you that I am he: if therefore ye seek me, let these go their way" (vv. 7-8).

Next, after Peter had severed the ear of the high priest's servant and after Jesus had healed it, "the band and the captain and officers of the Jews took Jesus and bound him" (v. 12). Could they have been mistaken about the identity of Jesus? Certainly not! Here are some reasons:

1. Of the disciples, no one knew Jesus better than Peter and John, and they followed him to the Palace of Caiaphas (John 18:15).
2. Altogether, during the period of his three denials, Peter lingered before a fire just outside the Palace of Caiaphas for "about the space of one hour" (Luke 22:59), and during that period he had a clear view of Jesus and what was going on.
3. After Peter's denials, and after the cock had crowed, the eyes of Jesus and Peter met, and Peter wept bitterly (22:62). Would Peter have wept if the accused had not been Jesus?
4. While Jesus was on the cross, many intimate friends had come to linger with him. Among these were John, Jesus' mother, Mary Magdalene, and Mary the wife of Cleophas. All of these people knew Jesus extremely well. If another had been crucified in

Jesus's place at least one of them would have made it known.
5. Many who stood by, including the chief priests who had just demanded his crucifixion, affirmed that Jesus of Nazareth was the one who was being crucified by mocking and saying, "He saved others; himself he cannot save" (Mark 15:31).
6. The thieves who were crucified with him also knew that he was Jesus of Nazareth. Indeed, one of the two requested that Jesus remember him when he came into his kingdom. See Luke 23:39-43.
7. Jesus' initial words on the cross: "Father, forgive them; for they know not what they do" (Luke: 23:34), also proved that he was Jesus of Nazareth, the Son of God; for, considering the circumstances, no one else could have forgiven a group that was being so illegal and unjustly cruel.
8. We must also acknowledge that nature realized that the one on the central cross was not a substitute for the Redeemer of humankind. The great darkness attested to by all four of the Evangelists confirms that. Also, Matthew added the graphic fact: "And behold the veil of the temple was rent in twain from the top to the bottom; and the earth did quake, and the rocks rent" (27:51; Mark 15:38-39; and Luke 23:47).
9. Finally, we have the word of the centurion who was in charge of the crucifixions: "Truly this was the Son of God" (Matt. 27:54).

* * *

With all these facts available, we have an open and shut case. *Jesus of Nazareth, God's only begotten Son, died on the cross in order to pay the penalty of our sins.* About that there can be no doubt!

Can You Answer?

1. Does the Koran (*Qur'an*) teach that Jesus was virgin-born?
2. Does the Koran teach that Jesus died on the cross?
3. What is the meaning of *grace*?
4. Give an acrostic of *grace*.
5. Could the supply of grace be diminished?
6. Give six reasons that assure us that it was Jesus of Nazareth who died on the cross.
7. What was the day and hour that Jesus was crucified?
8. What time was the great darkness? How long did it last?
9. What time did Jesus die?

3 A Rich Man's Tomb

Using the facts available, let's take a few moments to imagine how the events surrounding Joseph's tomb unfolded those many centuries ago.

As Joseph of Arimathea stood near the cross during the world-wide darkness, he was nervous about the time. As a rich Sadducee and member of the Sanhedrin, he was aware of Jewish law, and as he watched the man whom he had secretly loved writhe on the central cross, he was concerned about the time his dreadful suffering would end, for he had determined that he would place the body of Jesus in his own tomb that had just been completed.

Moses' words kept hammering in his mind: "[A convict's] body shall not remain all night upon the tree, but thou shalt in any wise bury him that day" (Deut. 21:23).

As a businessman Joseph knew that time was of the essence—that Jesus' remains had to be buried before sunset, the beginning of the Sabbath. He also knew that before he could place the body in his tomb he would have to deal with several overwhelming obstacles.

First, to touch the remains without permission from Pontius Pilate would be illegal. Moreover, he realized that Pilate was temperamental and as stubborn as Beelzebub. When the chief priests objected to the title he had written that boldly stated in Hebrew, Latin, and Greek JESUS OF NAZARETH THE KING OF THE JEWS, and ordered it placed on the cross, Pilate was inflexible. Thrusting out his stubborn chin he had snapped: "What I have written I have written" (John 19:19-22).

Joseph also realized that in order to give Jesus a royal burial, the kind he deserved, he would need to buy the necessary cloth and spices. Moreover, these tasks would not be easy, for Jerusalem was crowded with pilgrims.

As these potential complications presented themselves, Joseph suddenly noticed a new look cross the face of one of the thieves. Then he heard him say to Jesus, "Lord, remember me when thou comest into thy kingdom" (Luke 23:42).

Joseph gulped at Jesus' immediate reply: "Today shalt thou be with me in paradise" (v. 43). Did Joseph grasp what Jesus meant by the words *today*? No one knows.

But as Joseph considered the meaning, he was startled by hearing Jesus shriek in a loud voice, "Father, into thy hands I commend my spirit" (v. 46). Then, as tears bathed Joseph's eyes, he noticed that Jesus' head had slumped forward.

Jesus' beard had barely touched his chest when the darkness disappeared and Joseph noted that the sun was halfway toward the horizon. This meant that the time was approximately 3 P.M. and that his time was extremely limited.

Moments later, as he was turning to leave, he sickened when he witnessed a pair of Roman soldiers approach the thieves and methodically break their legs with a few swift blows. Having been present at other crucifixions, Joseph knew that this procedure had been ordered to hasten their deaths. The subtle meaning was that time was rushing by.

Next, while gritting his teeth, he watched the soldiers approach Jesus. At the base of the cross, they stared upward into his eyes, now wide from the pain he had suffered.

"He's already dead," shrugged the older one as he started to leave.

Without replying, his companion jabbed a lance into his side. Immediately water and blood gushed out.

Biting his lip at this sign of death, Joseph headed toward the Praetorium in order to see Pilate. As he elbowed through the crowds on this approximately half-mile journey, a series of problems pounded his heart. *What would he do if Pilate were not there, or refused to see him?* (That was a possibility, for his wife had cautioned him about condemning Jesus).

Or what would he do if Pilate remembered that the law forbade giving the body of a crucified victim to anyone, unless that person were a relative, and that giving the body to anyone, even a relative was completely illegal, if the victim had been condemned for sedition.

Joseph realized that he was not a relative of Jesus, and that Jesus had been condemned for sedition. *What should he do? He would trust that the providence of God would intervene!*

As he neared the Praetorium, he felt a tap on the shoulder. Turning, his eyes widened. "Nicodemus!" he exclaimed.

Nicodemus smiled. "Where are you going?" he asked.

"To see Pilate. I need permission to bury the body of Jesus."

"But do you have time to get permission and also prepare his corpse?" Nicodemus asked.

"Maybe you can help me," replied Joseph, impulsively. "We'll need spices and cloth. Why don't you get the cloth and spices?"

"And where should I take them?"

"To my new tomb. You know where it is. It's in a garden outside the walls where I've been raising flowers and vegetables. You can make sure that it's my tomb by checking with the gardener. He looks something like Jesus...."

"You mean the tomb near where they crucified him?"

"That's right."

"I'm on my way," replied this respected Pharisee, a ruler of the Jews, who had previously had an interview with Jesus at night. (See John 3:1-21.)

Nicodemus turned to leave.

Joseph held up his hand. "Before you leave, I want you to agree with me in prayer. Matthew, the tax collector—one of the Twelve—told me that he heard Jesus say: 'if two of you shall agree on earth as touching anything that they shall ask, it shall be done for them of my Father which is in heaven' " (18:19).

Nicodemus chuckled. "If Jesus said that, I know it's true, for he was truly the Son of God. I saw him open blind eyes and even raise the dead!" He placed his hand on Joseph's shoulder and peered deep into his eyes. "On what shall we agree?"

"That I get to see Pilate and that Pilate will give me permission to entomb the body of Jesus."

"But you know the law." Nicodemus looked doubtful. "You are neither a relative of Jesus; and, innocent though he was, he was crucified for sedition."

"Yes, yes I know. But Jesus said that if we are agreed, we can ask *anything*, 'and it shall be done.' Think of that. *Anything!*"

Joseph and Nicodemus joined hands. Each prayed separately for the requests Joseph had mentioned. At the conclusion of their petitions, Joseph said, "Now, Nicodemus, be generous with the spices and the cloth. Remember, we are burying royalty!"

Because of the rapidly sinking sun, Joseph quickened his pace. As he neared the Gentile building, he felt his heart thumping beneath his gown. Upon reaching the Pavement where Jesus had faced Pilate, he noticed the lines of a game cut into one of the wider pavement stones. As he glanced at it, he wondered if the soldiers who had gambled for Jesus' robe at the cross had also gambled here. With effort, he pushed these thoughts from his mind, and faced one of the guards. "I have an urgent need to see Pontius Pilate," he said.

"He's busy," replied the man as he fidgeted with his spear.

"I'm a member of the Sanhedrin," explained Joseph, lifting his voice a trifle. "Tell the procurator that my problem can be dealt with in a moment and that it is extremely important."

Moments later, Pilate appeared. "Yes, what can I do for you? Do you have someone else you want crucified?" His tone quivered with sarcasm.

"I-I would like to bury the body of Jesus."

"Are you related?" Pilate scowled.

"N-no."

"Mmmm. You know the law?"

"Yes, I know the law."

"You're not related. He was crucified for sedition. He claimed to be a king . . ."

"True, but . . ."

Pilate ran a hand over his freshly cropped hair.

As Joseph waited he could almost hear the beat of his own speeding heart.

"It would be a great favor," he ventured.

"Mmmm. Mmmm. Well, all right," he said. "But you'll have to get busy; the sun's nearing the horizon."

Joseph thanked him and hurried back to Golgotha. There, he was just in time to watch the final removal of Jesus's body from the cross. Placing the body on a cart, he motioned for a servant to help. Then, together, they headed toward the tomb. A few minutes later, Nicodemus, together with carryout workers from the store where he had purchased the linen cloth and spices, showed up with his purchases.

"How much do the spices weigh?" asked Joseph.

"About one hundred pounds." (John 19:39-40.)

"And what kind are they?"

"Myrrh and aloes."

Joseph smiled even though he knew that the price of the myrrh and aloes would dig deep into his resources. The bitter aloes was useful for embalming and the perfume excreted by the myrrh would fill the tomb with mystic perfume for months.

"It is strange," commented Nicodemus, "that when the Wise Men from the East visited Jesus at the time of his birth, they presented him with gold, frankincense, and myrrh. And now, although he does not have any gold, he's being buried with myrrh—a large quantity of myrrh, and—" (Matthew 2:11).

"We'd better stop visiting and get busy," interrupted Joseph. "Rigor mortis will soon stiffen the body. We must close his eyes and adjust his arms and legs while they're still pliable." Having done this, they kept the eyes closed by placing a heavy coin over each one. Next, they gently washed the body and cleansed the deep wound in the side. After this, they saturated strips of cloth in the spices and wound them around the arms and legs. (The linen cloth was from the most expensive bolt the merchant had on display. The threads were handmade. The finished product, also made by hand, had been woven in three-to-one herringbone twill.)

As they prepared the shroud, the conversation drifted onto the subject of the resurrection. "I know about the doctrines of the Sadducees," said Nicodemus, "and this is no time to argue. But do you *really* believe that this body we are preparing will be resurrected on the third day?"

Joseph was thoughtful as he positioned the hands. "That thought is a troubling one," he confessed, "for I believe that everything Jesus said is true. One day my old tax collector Matthew—he gave up that business to follow Jesus—said to me, "The Scribes and the Pharisees—no reflection on you, Nicodemus!—were always pressing Jesus for a sign. Once after Jesus had wearied of their insistence for a sign, he said to them: "An evil and adulterous generation seeketh after a sign; and there shall no sign be given to it, but the sign of the prophet Jonas: For as Jonas was three days and three nights in the whale's belly; so shall the Son of man be three days and three nights in the heart of the earth" (12:39-40).

"That means that Jesus will be resurrected from the dead," replied Nicodemus.

Joseph shrugged. "Yes, I guess that's what he meant . . ."

"But does the Bible really teach the resurrection of the dead?" pressed Nicodemus.

Joseph squirmed. "Maybe—maybe it does. B-b-but . . ." A faint smile smudged his face.

"What about Job's question, 'If a man die, shall he live again?' (14:14). During a moment of confidence, Job answered his own question: 'For I know that my redeemer liveth, and that he shall stand at the latter day upon the earth: and though after my skin worms destroy this body, yet in my flesh shall I see God' (19:25-26). Other examples come to mind."

"Give me one!" challenged Joseph.

"Here are several. 'Many of them that sleep in the dust of the earth shall awake, some to everlasting life, and some to shame and everlasting contempt' (Dan. 12:2). Another is in Psalm 16:10-11: 'For thou wilt not leave my soul in hell; neither wilt suffer thine Holy One to see corruption. Thou wilt show me the path of life: in thy presence is fullness of joy; at thy right hand there are pleasures for evermore.' Or what about Isaiah 26:19? There, the prophet said, 'Thy dead men shall live, together with my dead body shall they arise. Awake and sing, ye that dwell in dust: for thy dew is as the dew of herbs, and the earth shall cast out the dead.' "

Joseph smiled. "I'm not equal to you in knowledge of the Bible. But the wise ones say that there is no life after death. Who are we to dispute them?" He pointed to the sun. "We'd better hurry." His eyes had widened with alarm.

He wrapped more cloth around the body and then added, "If Jesus really rises from the dead, it will change all our beliefs." Then he asked, "Have you noticed those women sitting by the tomb? Who are they and why are they watching us so closely?" He jerked his thumb in their direction.

Nicodemus nodded but made no comment.

Years later, that question was answered by Matthew in the Gospel that bears his name: "And there was Mary Magdalene, and the other Mary, sitting over against the sepulchre" (27:61). Mark also, provided an answer: "Mary Magdalene and Mary the mother of Joses beheld where he was laid" (15:47). Luke's answer indicated that in addition to the two Marys there may have been other women: "And the women also, which came with him from Galilee, followed after, and beheld the sepulchre, and how his body was laid" (23:55).

While the shadows were lengthening, Joseph and Nicodemus placed the body in the tomb. The next problem was to roll the stone in place. The stone was probably perfectly flat, from six or eight feet in diameter, and at least a foot thick.

"We can't do it by ourselves," remarked Nicodemus.

"That's right," replied Joseph. "I'll summon the gardener."

The three men pried the stone upright and slowly rolled it toward the tomb. When they reached the wide groove by the door, they easily rolled it forward and closed the opening.

While they were pushing the stone, they noticed that the women were watching rather closely. "I-I w-wonder why they're so interested?" asked Nicodemus, breathing heavily. Joseph smiled. "I don't know."

Satisfied with their work, they left the sepulchre and walked together through the garden. "Why do you have so many lentils?" asked Nicodemus, lifting his voice.

"Because I like them," replied Joseph. "After you've eaten a dish of red pottage made of lentils, you can understand why Esau was willing to trade his birthright for a mess of them."[1] (See Gen. 25:29-34.) A large section was filled with mint.[2] Beside it were rows and rows of other vegetables and fruit, including various kinds of melons.

"Do you tithe the mint?" teased Nicodemus (Matt. 23:23).

"Of course! I also tithe my cummin." He pointed to a patch of the foot-high plant. "Cummin is good for all kinds of dishes—makes an excellent spice. Mmmm! My wife's a great cook. She puts it in her bread, and she wouldn't make a pot of meat without a pinch of it."

As they neared the edge of the garden, bordered with high yellowing mustard plants, they came to a fork in the road. "I guess we must part." Joseph held the hand of Nicodemus in both of his and warmly embraced him. "I'll probably see you at the temple tomorrow if the crowd isn't too large. And then we'll learn whether or not Jesus rises from the dead." He hesitated. "You know that it could be that Jesus wants us to take his statement about his resurrection spiritually. . . ."

"You may be right," conceded Nicodemus. "I do know that he was speaking in spiritual terms when he told me that I couldn't see the kingdom of God unless I was born again." He waved. "We'll soon find out. Sunday will be the third day!"

As Joseph of Arimathaea hurried home, did he have any idea that he had fulfilled Isaiah's prophecy: "He made his grave with the wicked, and with the rich in his death?" (53:9). Probably not.

* * *

Can You Answer?

1. Why did Joseph have to go to Pilate?
2. What were Jesus' last words on the cross?
3. When did the world-wide darkness disappear?
4. Why did the women go to the tomb?
5. What was the shape of the stone in front if the tomb?
6. How was the cloth used in the shroud woven?
7. What was the main doctrinal difference between the Sadducees and the Pharisees?

4 A Day in Old Jerusalem

The last three hours on Friday evening, April 7, the 14th of Nisan, A.U.C. 784, that stretched between 3 and 6 P.M., are among the most important hours in the history of humankind. For during those final 180 minutes Joseph of Arimathea along with Nicodemus placed the body of Jesus in his own, freshly hewn tomb.

But that was just one of the historic events that took place on that solemn day while the sun slowly sank toward the horizon.

As we review the situation, we know that the body of Jesus was in the tomb. Still, Jesus had made a promise to a thief. Did Jesus keep that promise?

We also know that women watched Joseph and Nicodemus prepare the body of Jesus. Why would they do that—especially on the eve of the Passover when there were other important tasks that needed to be done? And why did the women hurry away?

Also, where was Judas and Mary the mother of Jesus?

There are biblical solutions to these questions. But we'll deal with these late Friday events and the scriptural answers in the next chapter. Why? Because prior to his crucifixion, as Jesus viewed Jerusalem, he sobbed out a statement the world can never forget.

> O Jerusalem, Jerusalem, thou that killest the prophets, and stonest them which are sent unto thee, how often would I have gathered thy children together, even as a hen gathereth her chickens under her wings, and ye would not! (Matt. 23:37).

What was Jerusalem like as Jesus swept his eyes over the Mount of Olives, Gethsemane, the Kidron Valley—and the legendary Tomb of Absalom? Why was it that the people were not willing to find refuge under the shadow of his wide and patient wings, in the manner of a hen providing refuge for her chicks?

As Jesus viewed the city, he was both aware of its sordid and glorious past, and also its sordid and glorious future. In like manner—only we must depend on books!—let's take a quick glance at Jerusalem from modern times, back through the days when it was founded. Then let us pause for a moment and both view—and smell!—the city as it was when Jesus stumbled beneath the weight of his cross on the Via Dolorosa.

* * *

While spinning the calendar back, the A.D. years get smaller and smaller. We smile when 1492 flicks by, for we remember dear old Columbus. Then we skid down to the years from 1187 to 1099. That's the period when the Crusaders ruled Palestine; and the Crusaders, proud of the symbol for Anno Domini, vigorously numbered their years with A.D.

But from 1099 down to 638, the symbol A.D. was replaced with A.H. The reason was that Palestine had come under the control of Islam. Their calendar began with the Hegira—flight of Mohammed from Mecca to Medina in A.D. 622. Thus, when Omar conquered Jerusalem in A.D. 638, the *official* year, at least to the Muslims in authority, was A.H. 16 (After Hegira).

Before the A.H. system, and continuing up to 525 A.D. the Roman world numbered years with the letters A.U.C. (Ab Urbe Condita). Those letters referred to the mythical founding of Rome in 753 B.C. But in 525 A.D., Dennis the Little, a monk, who was skilled in figures, split the centuries into B.C. and A.D. The B.C. means Before Christ and A.D. means Anno Domini—in the year of the Lord. This system was used in the West after 525.

In the Jerusalem we will be visiting, the A.U.C. system was accepted by the Romans and a few others but certainly not by all. Indeed, there were so many calendars in Jerusalem, it was easy to get confused. Pious Jews had two sets: one of the civil year—and one for the religious year. Instead of going back to the founding of Rome, they went back—and still do—to the day of creation. Thus, in the Jewish world, this year, 1991, is 5752. The Jewish year was a lunar one; but since the lunar year lags behind the solar year, they had difficulty in staying even with the seasons. Their months were *Nisan, Yiar, Sivan, Tamuz, Ab, Elul, Tsiri Hesvan, Kislev, Tebet, Sebat,* and *Adar*. Passover was celebrated on the 15th of Nisan. This produced a problem since the earliest ears of barley had to be ready for the Passover. The barley, however, was not always ready because of the accumulation of the eleven-day lag each year.

To correct this, a thirteenth month, Yeadar, was slipped in every once in a while. But the Samaritans refused to recognize the extra month when it was decreed in Jerusalem. Instead, they named one to suit themselves. In addition to this confusion, the Greek cities insisted in following the calendar introduced to them by Alexander the Great!

To be absolutely clear, we will not follow any of these calendars during our visit. Instead, we will go sometime during the fifteenth year of the reign of Tiberius Caesar.

This is the year Jesus was baptized in the river Jordan.

* * *

The home in which we'll stay will depend on our pocketbook. (If it were during Passover, there would be no rent.) Jerusalem was crowded with the magnificent palaces of the Roman rulers, the rich, and the high priest. But it also had filthy hovels as well as modest places occupied by the middle class.

The home in which Simon Peter may have lived probably consisted of several rooms with a roof sloped just enough to carry off the rain. There may or may not have been a kitchen. Many preferred to cook outside, and during inclement weather inside a lean-to. The roof provided a place to rest, enjoy the breezes, and to get away from it all.

During our stay we will live in a home such as this.

Normally the Jews ate two meals a day—one early in the morning and the other after the day's work was done. As we prepare for the first meal, we must wash. The minimum washing required was that of just the right hand. Some bathed their entire bodies.

Food was served at a table and we must eat sitting down. Wealthy Jews, however, often ate while reclining on a couch. Following a blessing, we will eat. There will, of course, be no bacon or fish without scales; and it is likely that there will be no eggs. Only the rich could afford eggs. But undoubtedly there will be bread, perhaps some fruit and vegetables, and a piece of ceremoniously clean fish.

Having eaten, we go outside. The city of Jerusalem in the first century had a population of 150,000. This means that it was crowded and the houses were jammed close together like a crowded shopping center; and since the Jews were not good architects—Solomon brought in foreigners to plan the details of the temple—they were not works of beauty.

Starting up the street, we find a message on the wall.

The language of the wall-announcement is in Aramaic—the common vernacular of the street. Natives of Jerusalem used at least three languages. Hebrew was the language of the pious, for this was the language of the Bible. Greek, however, was used by the educated, for since the invasion of Alexander the Great, Greek had been the language of the well-read, just as English today is the popular language of the well-read in India and other countries formerly ruled by Great Britain.

The rabbis, however, loathed Greek. They considered it the language of sin. Some even said: "The man who teaches his son Greek is as accursed as the man who eats pork." Nonetheless, most of them understood Greek!

As we study the wall announcement, which turns out to be a warning from Pontius Pilate, a rank odor like that of burning flesh comes to us. We're about to inquire the reason when we notice crowds surging down the twisting and narrow streets. Most of the men have long hair and full beards and some of the younger set have their hair sprinkled with gold dust. Long coats and longer cloaks—they double as overcoats and sometimes blankets—are seen everywhere. Few of these billowing "blankets" fit well, and so they are secured around waists with beautiful belts.

The streets are mostly named after the gates to which they lead or to the larger bazaars that they pass or service. Thus there is *Water-Street, Fish-Street, Timber-Bazaar, Butcher-Street, Strangers'-Street, Braziers'-Bazaar,* and so forth.

As we continue down streets that make sudden turns to the left or right, we have a distinct feeling that we're about to get lost—and this is especially so when we are in streets that have not been named.

The rhythmic clip-clop of donkey hoofs fills the air, and we have to leap suddenly out of the way when a man sitting sideways on a donkey goes rushing by. We had expected to see animal-drawn carts; but we don't see many, for the simple reason that the streets are far too narrow to accommodate them. We do, however, notice a number of rich men who are being rushed down the streets in fancy litters carried on the shoulders of slaves. Soon we notice tight groups of animals being driven down the streets by fierce-eyed men with something obviously on their minds. Since they seem headed for a vital place, we follow them, believing we'll get to see something really important.

Soon we're in a nest of little shops, and here in a swarming bazaar we pause to look. The chatter of a dozen languages clash in our ears, and we observe all sorts of nationalities pressing up to the counters and fingering the merchandise. Displayed before us is a colorful variety of jewelry, baskets, pots and lamps, and other items we can't identify.

Since we need a souvenir, we buy a tiny lamp from a toothless old man who is blind in one eye. After handing him a silver denarius featuring the head of Tiberius Caesar, we pocket the copper mites of change.

As we wonder what happened to the animals we were following, we notice a horde of weeping people following a litter. Upon closer examination, we discover that the man in the litter is dead and that it is a funeral.

The procession is being led by a woman. A rabbi explains, "Since Eve brought death into the world, it's only right that women should lead death's victims to the grave." We watch the mourners as they head for a gate that pierces the wall. Then we start following another group of animals that seem headed in the direction of the previous group we saw earlier.

Soon we are facing the breath-taking temple that the Herods have been building. As we view it along with the various buildings connected with it, we are overwhelmed. Sublimely majestic with towers and lofty marble pillars, we forget the rat-like maze from which we've just emerged.

The new temple, together with its accompanying buildings, covers nearly thirty-five acres. Although not completed, it was already one of the wonders of the world. Proud rabbis liked to say: "The world is like an eye; the ocean surrounding the world is the white of an eye; its black is the world itself; the pupil is Jerusalem; but the image within the pupil is the sanctuary."

As our eyes widen, we agree that is an apt description.

Here we notice a huge gathering of animals—thousands of animals. As we watch, a sandaled Roman soldier strides up, for their barracks are at the nearby Antonia Fortress. Pointing to the clouds of smoke swirling upward, we ask, "Why all the smoke?"

"Oh, the Jews are making their sacrifices," he sighs as he throws out his hands in a gesture of despair. "They never seem to finish. Sometimes when the wind is just right the smoke seeps through my window and I nearly choke."

"Will all those animals be sacrificed?"

"Certainly, and a lot more."

(During the reign of Nero, the number of lambs slaughtered at a single Passover was 265,000. By multiplying that number by ten—the minimum total that could partake of a sacrificed lamb—more than two million were estimated to have attended that one Passover.)

But it's getting late and we must be at our lodgings before sunset, for that will be the beginning of the Sabbath and we don't want to embarrass our host by being on the street during those sacred hours.

Miraculously we find our way back while it is still daylight. Now we're glad that we can do a thorough job of scrubbing, for the sight of the animals and the smoke has made us feel both miserable and dirty. Fortunately, our host has a large supply of ashes. Using a handful, we scrub at the basin.

Soon three stars appear in the sky and then a series of sharp blasts from a ram's horn indicate that a new Sabbath has begun. The new Sabbath means that everyone should stop working and Jerusalem—all of Jerusalem—obeys.

Moses had taught that the Sabbath was the Lord's Day.

"Does this mean that I can't go for a walk tomorrow?, I inquired.

"If you were a Jew you should not walk more than a Sabbath day's journey, that is, two thousand cubits [about three thousand feet], but since you're a Gentile, you're not bound by that law." He thoughtfully rubbed his beard. "Nonetheless, if I were you, I'd be careful." He lifted his brows. "You might be stoned."

"Will I be able to go out and eat?"

The host smiled. "There will be no need for you to try to find an eating place. Since you're our guest, we will stay home, and we will eat well." He laughed. "Also, we'll put on our best clothes. Today is a day of rest—and happiness."

After a sumptuous meal, I turned to the host. "Give

me a short history of Jerusalem up to this time," I said.

"If I went into detail, I'd take a week. But here are the highlights." (To make this clear we'll put B.C. figures in the mouth of the host.)

"King David made Jerusalem the capital during his reign from 1000 to 961. During Solomon's reign—961-922—the first temple was built. At the end of his reign, the kingdom was divided between Israel [the Northern Kingdom] and Judah [the Southern Kingdom]. Solomon spent too much money!

"In 587 Nebuchadnezzar destroyed both our city and the temple. He exiled our people into Babylon," he laughed. "It was during the exile we learned to become businessmen!

"In 537 King Cyrus allowed us to return to Jerusalem. The second temple, known as Zerubbabel's Temple was completed in 516."

"Why, then, is Herod's Temple called the second temple? Shouldn't it be called the third temple?" I asked.

"Good question. The answer is that Zerubbabel's Temple could in no way be compared to Solomon's Temple. Zerubbabel merely repaired it!" He shrugged.

"We must hurry and so we'll skip a few dates. The Ptolemies ruled from 312 to 198. Then the Seleucids took over and reigned until 167. They were vicious. Antiochus Epiphanes [175-163], forbade circumcision. Women who disobeyed were crucified and their circumcised son was hanged around her neck while she perished on the cross. Antiochus also sacrificed a pig on our holy altar!

"Judas Maccabees finally got rid of the Seleucids in 141. After that Jerusalem was captured by the Roman general Pompey in 63. He was followed by the Caesars, Augustus—and now Tiberius.

"Do you want me to tell you anymore?"

"No thanks. It'll take me a long time to digest what I've already heard. But I must make one comment. The Jews must be a hardy people to endure all this—and yet survive."

"Yes, we are a both a rugged and determined nation. But there is a reason. We are the children of Abraham!" He spoke slowly and emphasized each word.

Tiberius Caesar was the emperor of Rome from A.D. 14-37. This means that he was on the throne at the time of the crucifixion. Although an apt ruler, he spent much of his time on the Isle of Capri. In a palace lined with pornographic paintings, he indulged in vice—especially that which involved children (Ludwig 1983). In his 79th year, Tiberius was allegedly smothered to death by Caligula who followed him as Roman Emperor in A.D. 37.

* * *

Can You Answer?

1. What is the meaning of A.U.C., A.D., B.C., and A.H.?
2. What was the name of the thirteenth month in the lunar year?
3. Who were the Caesars who ruled in Jesus' lifetime?
4. What kind of fish were forbidden to the Jews?
5. How many meals did Jews normally eat in one day?
6. How long was a Sabbath day's journey?
7. Did the Rabbis appreciate the Greek language?
8. What was the normal population of Jerusalem?
9. What day of the week was the Jewish Sabbath?

5 Friday Evening

Considering the numerous calendars in use in Jerusalem and the fact that the Jewish day was from sunset to sunset rather than from midnight to midnight as in our system, it's confusing to try and decide which day and which time in a Jewish month a certain event took place.

If we want a sharp picture of an incident, it's necessary to be able to accurately translate the time from one system into a system we understand. Similarly, when driving in a country that uses the metric system, it's important to be able to translate miles into kilometers and kilometers into miles.

This fact was brought forcibly to me in 1958 when I went to Kenya to perform my parents' fiftieth wedding ceremony. On that occasion, when a native pastor asked me the time I would preach for them, I said, "I'll be with you at seven o'clock."

Unfortunately, the pastor forgot that I knew their

language—and their biblical time system, and so instead of gathering at 1 P.M. as I meant, they came at 7 A.M!

Realizing this difficulty, Giovanni Rosadi, in his *Trial of Jesus*, printed a chart that shows the days of the Passion Week both in the month of April and Nisan. Here it is:

April 2, Sunday—	Up to sunset.	Nisan 9.
	After sunset.	Nisan 10.
April 3, Monday—	Up to sunset.	Nisan 10.
	After sunset.	Nisan 11.
April 4, Tuesday—	Up to sunset.	Nisan 11.
	After sunset.	Nisan 12.
April 5, Wednesday—	Up to sunset.	Nisan 12.
	After sunset.	Nisan 13.
April 6, Thursday—	Up to sunset.	Nisan 13.
	After sunset.	Nisan 14.
April 7, Friday—	Up to sunset.	Nisan 14.
	After sunset.	Nisan 15.
April 8, Saturday—	Up to sunset.	Nisan 15.

(Rosadi 1905, 127).

By this chart we can see that the Last Supper, the arrest, the crucifixion, and the entombment, all took place on Nisan 14; or, in our calendar, the Last Supper was on Thursday evening, April 6 and the trial, crucifixion, and entombment were on Friday April 7. The year was 783 A.U.C. or—considering the mistake made by Dennis the Little—A.D. 29.

Before we consider what happened during the last three hours on Friday, April 7, Nisan 14, we must consider the whereabouts of Judas Iscariot. This is so, for his final actions undoubtedly took place *before* those concluding hours just prior to the beginning of the Jewish Sabbath. That is, they took place prior to the 15th of Nisan, which began at sunset on Friday.

Those who have tried to be sympathetic with Judas like to point out that he was the only one of the Twelve who was not a Galilean. Instead, he was from Kerioth—twenty miles south of Jerusalem and fifteen miles west of the Dead Sea.

Undoubtedly this son of Simon Iscariot (John 6:71) was the loneliest of the men who followed Jesus. Not related to any in the group, he did not feel at home. True, he was trusted as the treasurer, but other than for the Last Supper and the betrayal, he apparently did not take part in any of the great scenes mentioned in the Gospels.

Judas Iscariot was a tragic victim of peer-pressure.

In the three lists of the Twelve in the Gospels, Judas dangles at the bottom, while Simon Peter is triumphantly comfortable at the top (Matt. 10:4; Mark 3:19; and Luke 6:16).

What could Judas do to attain the recognition he deserved? The answer was clear. He could put Jesus on the spot and force him to establish the earthly kingdom all the patriots in Israel passionately longed to see.

How else can we answer the betrayal? The thirty pieces of silver he received for identifying Jesus weren't much. They were merely the amount a slave could receive if his master beat him until he bled. *Perhaps*, reasoned Judas, *if I force his hand he will demonstrate his power by tossing the Romans into the sea.*

Did Judas think that Jesus would actually be crucified? Certainly not! After all, his leader had the power to raise the dead! Early that morning when Jesus was arrested, Judas was probably more surprised than anyone. Since Judas was hoping that Jesus would perform a miracle, his face must have firmed with fanatical enthusiasm when, after Jesus had identified himself to the arresting mob, the mob—including Judas—"went backward, and fell to the ground" (John 18:6).

Rising from the ground, together with the arresting officers, Judas undoubtedly concluded that his little scheme of putting Jesus onto the spot was working. Soon he had two more throbs of encouragement. One was when Peter drew his sword and slashed off the ear of Malchus, the servant of the high Priest; the other was when Jesus touched the servant's ear and healed him (Luke 22: 51). *Perhaps Peter's action, and Jesus' miracle would convince the mob, and they would swear their loyalty, arrest the Roman authorities, and set up a theocracy. Then Jesus would immediately inaugurate his kingdom—a kingdom that would far surpass that of Solomon or even David.*

For a moment Judas was ecstatic.

Alas, as he watched, Jesus allowed himself to be bound with ropes and to be led away. Sickened at this turn of events, Judas followed the arresting officers and their prisoner. Perhaps at the right moment Jesus would snap the ropes, take command, and declare the Jewish nation free from the Roman yoke.

But Jesus refused to blink an eye in order to free himself.

Sick at heart, Judas' face tensed and he bit his lip. John related the rest of the story: "When they had bound him, they led him away, and delivered him to Pontius Pilate the governor. Then Judas, which had betrayed him, when he saw that he was condemned, repented himself, and brought again the thirty pieces of silver to the chief priests and elders, Saying, I have sinned in that I have betrayed the innocent blood. And they said, What is that to us? see thou to that. And he cast down the pieces of silver in the temple and departed, and went and hanged himself" (Matt. 27:2-5).

Alas, even in his suicide, Judas miscalculated. In his desperate hurry, he tied a rope to the limb of a tree, secured the noose around his neck—and leaped off a cliff. Apparently the limb broke, for Luke wrote: "Falling headlong, he burst asunder in the midst, and all his bowels gushed out" (Acts 1:18).

But that miscalculation wasn't his worst! His worst miscalculation was that although he repented, he failed to go to Christ and plead forgiveness. A single look would have been sufficient! Had he done so, the New Testament might contain a twenty-eighth book—The Gospel According to Saint Judas!

* * *

Now we must return to the cross. While Jesus was hanging there, suspended by the nails in his hands and feet, he focused his eyes on his mother; and then after moistening his lips, he whispered in a voice just loud enough to be heard above the taunts of the mob, "Woman, behold thy son!" Then he turned to John and added, "Behold thy mother!" (John 19:26-27).

John tells us "From that hour that disciple took her unto his own home" (v. 27).

Without a doubt, John and Mary lingered at the cross until after Jesus had cried "It is finished" (v. 30).

Soon, however, perhaps after Joseph of Arimathea had indicated that he would bury the remains of Jesus, John took Mary into his own Jerusalem home. That was indeed an agonizing ordeal for both of them, and especially Mary. We can easily imagine her slumped in a chair and wiping her eyes. Likewise, we can easily imagine her muttering between sobs,

"He was *such* a good boy. . . . He never caused trouble. . . . He liked to sit up late while I mended clothes. . . . I still remember how he often urged me to go to bed. He'd say, 'Mother, you need your rest.' I could always count on Jesus!"

Later, after it seemed that she could not shed another tear, one can almost see a new light brightening her eyes, and hear her reminisce: "I will never forget when the angel Gabriel came to me and said, 'Fear not Mary: for thou hast found favour with God. And behold, thou shalt conceive in thy womb, and bring forth a son, and shalt call his name JESUS' " (Luke 1:31).

Mary wiped her eyes again, and then in a moment of control, murmured, "He said that he would arise from the grave on the third day. D-d-do y-you believe that?"

"Yes, I-I try to believe it," replied John, forcing himself to be optimistic.

But where was Jesus during those three hours? On the cross he had assured the thief, "Today shalt thou be with me in paradise" (Luke 23:43). Did he keep that promise? He most assuredly did! This means that immediately after he cried, "It is finished" Jesus was in paradise. Ah, but where is paradise?

This is a problem many commentators skip. Even so, Gleason Archer had the courage to discuss it in his *Encyclopedia of Bible Difficulties*. Here is his solution:

"Jesus apparently refers to [paradise] in the parable of the rich man and Lazarus as 'Abraham's Bosom,' to which the godly beggar Lazarus was carried by the angels after his decease (Luke 16:19-31). Thus Abraham's Bosom referred to the place where the souls of the redeemed waited until the day of Christ's resurrection. Presumably this was the same place as paradise. It was not yet lifted up to heaven but it may well have been a section of hades . . . reserved for believers who had died in the faith but who would not be admitted into the glorious presence of God in heaven until the price of redemption actually had been paid on Calvary.

"Doubtless it was to paradise that the souls of Jesus and the repentant thief repaired after they each died on Friday afternoon" (Archer 1982, 387).

Gleason clinches his argument with statements by Paul: "We read in Ephesians 4:8 concerning Christ:

'Ascending on high, He lead captivity captive, and gave gifts unto men.' Verse 9 continues: 'But what does "He ascended" mean but that he also descended to the lowest parts of the earth?'—i.e. to hades.

"Verse 10 adds: 'He who descended is the same as He who ascended above all the heavens.' Presumably, He led the whole band of liberated captives from hades (i.e., the whole population of preresurrection paradise) up to the glory of the highest heaven, the abode of the Triune God" (Archer 1982, 368).

Since Jesus died before the thief died, he was in paradise in time to greet him just as he entered. How did he greet him? No one knows, but surely he must have greeted him with his nail-scarred hands—hands that carried within them the receipt of the thief's salvation, and that of the utter cleansing of his sins.

* * *

Joseph of Arimathea and Nicodemus were puzzled by the presence of the women at the tomb as they prepared the body of Jesus. Who were those women, and why did they come to the sepulchre? Matthew mentioned "Mary Magdalene and the other Mary." Mark indicated that they were "Mary Magdalene and Mary the mother of Joses." Luke did not name these two, but he said "The women also which came from Galilee, followed after and beheld the sepulchre." (23:55). That word *also* must include Mary Magdalene and Mary the mother of Joses. Nevertheless the names of all the Galilean women are unknown.

But before we try to find out *why* they were at the sepulchre as the body was being prepared by Joseph, we must identify those whose names we know.

The first one we will consider is Mary Magdalene. This Mary, a native of Magdala—a little town just west of the Sea of Galilee—is one of the most misunderstood women in the New Testament. Luke referred to her as the woman "out of whom went seven devils" (8:2). From this statement she has been identified with the woman described in Luke 7:36-50. Luke did not name this earlier woman. Instead, he described her as "a woman in the city, which was a sinner." Likewise, he related how she washed the feet of Jesus with her tears, wiped them with her hair, and then anointed them with expensive ointment from an alabaster box. This woman, dubbed a sinner, was presumed to be a prostitute.

But Luke's reference to "Mary called Magdalene" came much later and in an entirely different situation. The woman who washed Jesus' feet was obviously another person. Moreover, the fact that seven devils were cast out of Mary Magdalene does not imply that she was a woman of the streets.

Numerous imaginative remarks are said about Mary Magdalene. However, there is also some solid scripture about her. For example, Luke mentions her along with other women who "ministered unto him of their substance" (8:2-3). Also, we know that she was at the cross during the crucifixion (Matt. 27:56).

But who was the other Mary, Mary the mother of Joses? This Mary is hard to identify. We know that she was one of the women from Galilee who viewed the crucifixion from a distance (Matt. 27:55-56). That passage also states that she was the "mother of James and Joses." But who were James and Joses? Matthew 13:55 and Mark 6:3 state that "James, and Joses, and . . . Judah and Simon" were the brothers of Jesus. Was this Joses, therefore, the brother of Jesus? Roman Catholics say no; for, believing in the perpetual virginity of Mary, they insist that the brothers and sisters mentioned in these passages were merely cousins of Jesus. We can only shrug. No one knows. The one fact we do know is that this Mary was a warm friend of Mary Magdalene.

What did these women say when, after watching Joseph of Arimathaea and Nicodemus prepare the body of Jesus, they started home. The New Testament is silent. But after being married for over half a century, I could imagine one saying to the other, "Those men did the best they could. But let's return to the sepulchre right after the Sabbath on the first day of the week and make certain that his shroud is just right."

Back at one of their homes, they began to prepare the sweet spices for the future anointing of the body just as they had planned. While they worked, a rabbi who had been searching the sky, noticed the third star, put the ram's horn to his lips, and sounded three shrill blasts.

Those ram's horn blasts signaled that it was now the Sabbath—the fifteenth of Nisan.

Immediately upon hearing it, all work in Jerusalem stopped. Putting down the spices, Mary Magdalene must have sighed, "We'll finish our preparation on the First Day of the week."

* * *

That night it was hard for those who had loved Jesus to concentrate on their Passover duties. The thought that dominated their minds was this: Our friend, was crucified. He's now lying all alone in a cold, cold tomb. What, oh what will we do?

* * *

Can You Answer?

1. What time did a Jewish day start and close?
2. Where was Judas Iscariot born?
3. What was the Gregorian year in which these events took place?

4. Why did Judas betray Jesus?
5. Where was Jesus after he had been placed in the tomb?
6. Where was Mary Magdalene born?
7. Was Mary Magdalene a prostitute?
8. Name two of Jesus brothers.
9. How many stars did a rabbi have to see before he signaled a new day?

6 Passover

Legend insists that the Virgin Mary spent several years of her girlhood in Jerusalem. True or false, we know that she visited the city at least once a year at Passover and was thus familiar with its walls, gates, main streets—and even some of its more obscure alleys.

Three visits to the Holy City for special occasions were mentioned in the New Testament. The first visit was when Jesus was forty days old. Its purpose was to obey Leviticus 12 for her purification and to present her son to the Lord. The requirement was either to submit a lamb for a burnt offering and a turtle dove for a sin offering, or, if the parents could not afford a lamb, a turtle dove for a burnt offering and another for a sin offering (Lev. 12:6, 8).

Luke explained the essential meaning of this visit: "They brought him to Jerusalem to present him to the Lord," (Luke 2:22).

The second visit was when Mary and Joseph took

Jesus to the temple at the age of twelve to celebrate Passover. This was the occasion when he was "lost." The story is in Luke 2:42-49.

Her final recorded visit was when Jesus was crucified.

Raised in Judaism, and being familiar with the temple, Mary understood the laws of Moses together with their many intricate complications. For example, after giving birth to Jesus, she was considered ceremoniously unclean for thirty-three days; but had Jesus been a girl, she would have been ceremoniously unclean for sixty-six days. (Leviticus 12:2-5).

From the time she was mature enough to understand, she learned the meaning of the feasts of Passover, Tabernacles, Unleavened Bread, New Moon, and so on. The Feast of Unleavened Bread starting together with the Passover on the fifteenth of Nisan was especially exciting. Early memories of the Feast of Unleavened Bread were permanently fixed in her mind. Every year her father with a lighted candle in hand, searched through all the closets, all the corners, and under all the beds in their house.

Before she understood the meaning of this strange behavior, Mary approached her father after he had blown out the candle.

"What are you doing?" she asked.

"I'm searching for leaven?" he replied, lifting her onto his lap.

"Why?"

"I'll explain that during Passover," he replied, kissing her on the cheek.

Waiting for Passover was extremely hard; but there were many activities going on in Jerusalem that whetted her curiosity.

"Why are they repairing all the roads and bridges?" she asked.

"Because there will be large crowds who will come to

Jerusalem for Passover. We don't want anyone to be inconvenienced by holes in the roads or broken-down bridges."

"Why are so many men carrying buckets of whitewash out to the cemeteries?"

"They're whitewashing all the tombs and sepulchers."

"Why?"

"Because when the pilgrims come to Jerusalem many will pitch their tents outside the city. If anyone touches a sepulchre or grave or that which is dead he'll be ceremoniously unclean and will not be able to enjoy the Passover Feast until he's cleansed. The whitewash is a warning."

(This custom may have inspired Jesus to compare the scribes and Pharisees to "whited sepulchers, which indeed appear beautiful outward, but are within full of dead men's bones." See Matthew 23:27.)

"Who said it was wrong to touch a grave or sepulchre?" persisted Mary, her eyes wide with curiosity.

"Moses."

"Why?"

"Oh, Mary. You ask too many questions! When you get a little older you'll understand the meaning of all these laws."

With that, her father went outside to make certain that his donkey had enough to eat.

A few days later, Mary rushed home from the temple. Eyes wide, she blurted: "I just saw a terrible thing."

"Yes?" asked her father.

"While I was at the temple I saw a priest take a man to a door and push an awl through his ear into the door. Ouch! It was awful." She shook her head.

Her father replied, "That priest was just following a law of Moses. I'll read his words from the book of Deuteronomy." He unwound the scroll to the right place. Then he said: "Our lawgiver taught that slaves should be set free after they've served seven years. But you see some slaves don't want to be freed. In such cases, Moses told us what to do. Listen! 'Then thou shalt take an awl, and thrust it through his ear unto the door, and he shall be thy servant for ever' " (15:17).

"I'm glad I was born free!" exclaimed Mary.

"And so are we," replied her father, patting her on her head.

Finally, after numerous other ceremonies, Mary's father said, "It's now the thirteenth day of Nisan, and this is a very important day." He picked up a candle. But before lighting it, he offered the following prayer: "Blessed art Thou, Jehovah, our God, King of the Universe, who has sanctified us by Thy commandments, and commanded us to remove the leaven."

Then, amidst strict silence, he made another thorough search for leaven. At the conclusion, he announced: "All the leaven that is in my possession, that which I have seen and that which I have not seen, be it null, be it accounted as the dust of the earth" (Edersheim 1950, 220).

(Dr. Edersheim suggested that the idea of searching with candles may have come from Zephaniah: "And it shall come to pass at that time, that I will search Jerusalem with candles" (1:12). He also pointed out that Paul may have been thinking of this custom when he wrote: "Purge out therefore the old leaven" (1 Cor. 5:7).

The Paschal lamb was always selected on the fourteenth of Nisan. This lamb had to meet stringent requirements. It had to be without blemish. It could not be younger than eight days and no older than one year. Also, it must not be from the tithe of lambs that had been selected for the Lord, nor was one permitted to offer the first lamb born to the flock.

Having been selected, the lamb was taken to the

temple. There, the owner of the lamb, together with a group of twenty-nine additional owners were admitted into the Court of the Priests. Having entered, the gates were bolted. At that moment, while the owners prepared to kill their Paschal lambs, the priests blew their silver trumpets three times.

After the three-fold blasts, and while the smoke of incense filled the air, each worshiper hurriedly killed the lamb he had brought. Next, the blood was drained into a golden bowl. This blood was then poured into a silver bowl and was relayed from one priest to another up to the altar. There, it was flung at the foot of the sacred place. While this was transpiring the priests sang the Hallel.

During the hymn, when the priests intoned hallelujah, the thirty worshipers, responded with the counterpart. Each hallelujah was answered with another hallelujah.

At the conclusion of this section of the ceremony, the lambs were suspended from hooks, skinned, and their entrails removed and cleaned. Next, the fat was placed in a dish, salted, and flung into the fire on the altar.

The rising smoke terminated the burnt offering.

The remaining part of the lamb was then taken home for the Passover Feast, which would be celebrated on the next day.

Passover celebrations increased in importance as the centuries passed. One reason was that the people were told that numerous historical events had taken place on the date of Passover. These events included the fall of Jericho, the destruction of Sodom, the writing on the wall in Babylon, the execution of Haman—and the sudden destruction of thousands of Assyrians who fought under the command of Sennacherib.

Such legends and mysteries were difficult for Jewish children to understand. But year after year, during the Passover Feast, the family were informed in a ritualistic ceremony the reason and cause for each part of the celebration. In this way, Mary eventually grasped the meaning of the unleavened bread and bitter herbs eaten during the feast, together with the reasoning behind the ritualistic slaying and eating of the sacrificial lamb.

While at home and amidst complicated ceremonies that included prayers, the washing of hands, the drinking of wine, and the breaking of the matzah (unleavened bread), the youngest child in the group stood and asked the Four Questions each of which was centered around the main one:

Why is this night different than all nights?

The leader of the ceremony then explained the meaning of Passover. Paul's teacher, Rabbi Gamaliel, urged them to do this by insisting: "Whoever does not explain three things in the Passover has not fulfilled the duty incumbent on him. These three things are: The Passover lamb, the unleavened bread, and the bitter herbs. The Passover lamb means that God passed over the blood sprinkled place on the houses of our fathers in Egypt. The unleavened bread means that our fathers were delivered out of Egypt (in haste); and the bitter herbs means that the Egyptians made bitter the lives of our fathers in Egypt" (237).

Abraham P. Bloch has detailed how the Paschal Lamb was to be eaten. "There were a number of restrictive rules attached to the feast. 'They shall eat the flesh in that night, roast with fire, and unleavened bread; and with bitter herbs shall they eat it' (Exod. 12:8). They were not to eat it rare or boiled in water (Exod. 12:9). They were not to leave the meat over past the conclusion of the night (Exod. 12:10). They were not to break any of the bones of the lamb (Exod. 12:46). No alien sojourner, hired servant, or uncircumcised person could eat the meat of the paschal lamb (Exod. 12:43-45). The feast was to be held in one house, and no part of the meat was to be taken outside the house (Exod. 12:46)" (Bloch 108).

(The biblical background for the Feasts of Passover and Unleavened Bread is found in Exodus 11—12.)

* * *

With this knowledge in her mind together with the memory of the many passovers, especially those within the time of the ministry of Jesus, Mary had many questions. Since John had taken her to "his own home" (19:27), the question arises: Did Mary celebrate the Passover with John and his circle of friends? This is a mystery, for we know that he, along with the other eleven disciples, had been guests at the Last Supper. That supper with Jesus had been on what we would deem to be Thursday during the early hours of the Jewish Friday—the fourteenth of Nisan. Was *that* meal *the* Passover Supper?

John informs us that what was obviously the final supper with the Twelve was "*before* the feast of the passover." (13:1). But the Synoptists refer to this "Last Supper" as the Passover. (See Matt. 26:17-19; Mark 14:12-16; and Luke 22:7-13.) How can this difference between John and the other Gospels be reconciled?

This conundrum has kept brilliant minds awake for centuries—and yet no one has produced a completely satisfactory solution. In the appendix to his book, *The Temple, Its Ministry and Service*, Edersheim quotes F. W. Farrar as speculating that the "Last Supper . . . was a quasi-Passover, a new Christian Passover" (Edersheim 1950, 390). But, after printing Farrar's views, Edersheim disagreed with them! Even so, many researchers think Farrar was right. Most scholars merely shrug.

Did Mary discuss the Last Supper with John? No one knows.

Strangely, the word *lamb* is not mentioned in the reports about the Last Supper by any of the Gospel writers. Nor did they refer to unleavened bread. Does this mean that Jesus and the Twelve did not have a roasted lamb, bitter herbs, or unleavened bread on this occasion?

Matthew, Mark, and Luke indicate that Jesus requested the disciples to prepare a *passover* feast. (Matt: 26:17-19; Mark 14:12-16; and Luke 22:7-13.) Mark stated that Jesus assigned this task to "two of his disciples" (v. 13). Luke is more specific. "He sent Peter and John saying, Go and make ready for us the passover, that we may eat" (v. 8).

But did those assigned to this task buy a lamb, bitter herbs, a supply of wine—and did they purchase or prepare unleavened bread? Let's look at the record.

Curiously, John did not mention any of the normal passover ingredients, nor did he mention the way Jesus instituted Holy Communion. Nonetheless, he used fourteen verses to describe the way Jesus washed the disciples' feet (13:4-17).

In contrast, the other three evangelists did not mention the foot-washing highlight, but all three mentioned the way Jesus instituted Holy Communion. Matthew's description fills three verses. Those of Mark and Luke each use four verses.

The betrayal is mentioned by all the writers. Only John, however, recorded Jesus' most specific identification: "He it is, whom I shall give the sop, when I have dipped it" (13:26). What constituted the sop? Edersheim had a definite opinion: "But we have direct testimony, that, at the time of Christ "the sop' which was handed round consisted of all these things wrapped together: flesh of the Paschal Lamb, a piece of unleavened bread, and bitter herbs. This we believe was the sop" (Edersheim n.d., 506).

Did John and Mary participate in the regular Passover Feast? Undoubtedly they did. But having suffered inexpressible grief, Mary had little or no appetite; and she made a hidden sigh of relief when the ceremonies were over.

Mary could hardly get to sleep. All through the night she could hear the thump, thump, thump of the hammers driving the nails: the taunting derision of the crowds; the statements of her eldest son, and his plaintive: "My God, my God, why hast thou forsaken me?" (Matt. 27:46).

She also had dreadful memories of his raw and harrowed back, his bruised and swollen face—and the crimson lines of blood that meandered from his hands and feet.

As mother of five sons and at least two daughters (Matt. 13:55-56), Mary was at least in her early forties—and that was old age for the time. Moreover, she was a widow. According to Jewish law, her eldest son was expected to support her. But now that Jesus was dead, how could this be possible? True, Jesus had turned that responsibility over to John. Nonetheless, now that John had been singled out as a close follower of Jesus, would he be financially capable of supporting her?

John and the Zebedees had been blessed with modest wealth. They employed servants (Mark 1:20). Zebedee's wife, Salome, and thus the mother of James and John, was one of the women who had supported Jesus, (Matt. 27:55-56; Mark 15:40-41, and Luke 8:2-3). But now that Jesus was dead, would the authorities allow them to keep their wealth?

Riches had a subtle way of disappearing!

Mary's worries were intensified by her memories of the crucifixion. She had seen the face of Caiaphas. His dark eyes were bright with hate; and his determined jaw indicated that he would not give up until even the memory of Jesus had been purged from the earth. By his manner, Mary was confident that he was already planning not only to eliminate Peter and John, but also to eliminate each of the Eleven.

Rolling and tossing, Mary found it impossible to keep such disturbing thoughts from haunting her very being. Once, when on the verge of sleep, she was awakened by the mournful howl of a nearby dog. On another occasion when she seemed about to slip into unconsciousness, she was awakened by the sound of marching feet. Terrified, she pushed the curtain aside and peered through the window.

Numb with fright, Mary stared at a group of fully armed Roman soldiers. *Who were they, and what did they want?* As she watched, they continued heading toward Calvary. Her eyes followed them until they disappeared around a turn in the road.

Suddenly Mary's thoughts were interrupted by the crowing of a cock. Its shrill greetings to the dawn meant time to get up. Thankful that morning had come, Mary slipped out of bed onto the cold floor.

While dressing she wondered why the soldiers were on the way to the place where her son had died. After all, this was the Sabbath. No one could be crucified on the Sabbath! Convinced that John would know, she hurriedly freshened her face, put on her sandals, combed her hair—and hurried downstairs.

As she opened the door, she noticed John and a number of others standing near the table. They were engaged in earnest conversation.

* * *

Can You Answer?

1. What does the word *passover* mean?

2. Where is the biblical background for the passover found?
3. How long have the Jews celebrated passover?
4. Why did Mary take Jesus to the temple when he was only forty days old?
5. What was the meaning of *unleavened bread*?
6. Why did Jewish authorities order the sepulchers to be whitewashed before the passover?
7. On what Jewish date was the passover celebrated?
8. Which Gospel writer mentioned the foot-washing service in the Upper Room?
9. Did John write about the way Jesus instituted the Lord's Supper?

7 The Longest Night

The moment there was a pause in the conversation, Mary burst out: "I-I just saw some soldiers! And they were headed t-toward the place where my son was crucified."

"We know all about it," replied a stranger whom she had never met. "While I was out walking a man explained the entire situation to me. He told me the chief priests and some Pharisees confronted Pilate. They said, 'Sir, we remember that the deceiver said . . . After three days I will rise again. Command therefore that the sepulchre be made sure until the third day, lest his disciples come by night, and steal him away, and say unto the people, He is risen from the dead: so the last error shall be worst than the first' " (Matt. 27:63-64).

"Pilate answered at once: 'Ye have a watch: go your way and make it as sure as you can.' In addition, he told them to seal it with a Roman seal."

"Does that mean that the soldiers I saw were members

of the watch that was sent to guard the tomb?" asked Mary.

"I think so," replied the stranger, pursing his lips.

Mary stared. Then she faced John. "Do you know of any plan to remove his body?"

"Certainly not!" John spoke with emphasis.

"When did Jesus say he would rise again?" asked Mary.

"On the third day," replied John.

Holding up his fingers, a man counted. "He was crucified yesterday on the fourteenth. Today is the fifteenth, and this evening at sunset will be the sixteenth. That means we're only a few hours from the third day!"

"Does that infer that he could rise from the dead tonight?" asked several all speaking at once.

"It does," put in John. "But remember, he didn't tell us at what time he would arise on the third day."

"M-maybe Jesus' statement was merely a parable," suggested a slender man who up to this time had been silent.

"Or maybe he was just speaking in figurative terms. As you know they accused him of saying 'I will destroy this temple that is made with hands, and within three days I will build another made without hands'" (Mark 14:58), remarked the stranger.

"He was undoubtedly speaking about his own body," replied John. Mary's guardian spoke with solemn authority. "I remember well the occasion when I first heard Jesus say that, and I remember that some scoffed: 'Forty and six years was this temple in building, and will thou raise it up in three days?' But Jesus was not referring to the temple built by Herod. He was referring to his own body" (John 2:19-21).

"Perhaps Jesus didn't mean that his own physical body would be resurrected. Maybe he meant that after three days his life and teachings would be remembered," proposed a short man as he scratched his cheek.

"We shall see. We shall see," replied the stranger. "But I doubt that you are right, for I remember when he raised Lazarus from the dead. He'd been dead four days. They had to remove his graveclothes so that he could walk." Inspired, he added, "Maybe they'll have to do that with Jesus!"

"Instead of speculating," cautioned another, "we should go to the temple. We don't want to miss the morning sacrifice."

* * *

As John accompanied Mary on the way to the temple, he noticed that her eyes were again overflowing. "What's bothering you?" he asked.

"I was thinking of the first time Joseph and I took Jesus to the temple. He was just a tiny baby, only forty days old—and now that son of mine is dead and is lying in a cold tomb. Oh, John, it's terrible, terrible, terrible . . ."

John slipped his arm around her. "Don't worry, Mary, Jesus is still alive," he comforted. "Jesus' words in the Upper Room keep coming back to me. After he had revealed that one of us would betray him, he became extremely troubled. Then with a sound of triumph and sorrow mixed together in his magnificent voice he said: 'Let not your heart be troubled: ye believe in God, believe also in me. In my Father's house are many mansions: if it were not so I would have told you. I go to prepare a place for you. And if I go to prepare a place for you, I will come again, and receive you unto myself; that where I am, there ye may be also' " (John 14:1-3).

As they approached the temple, Mary and John passed numerous people who had been healed by Jesus. All their faces were etched with lines of deep concern.

"If they were to reveal their thoughts," whispered John to Mary as he nodded at a former blind man, "and their words got to Caiaphas, they might be arrested. I'm dreadfully concerned about Jesus' followers, and especially about Peter and myself. Being in the fish business, the Zebedees are well known to many of those who demanded that Jesus be crucified."

* * *

Services in the temple were punctual. Since in lowlying places like Jericho and loftier places like Jerusalem, sunset was not observed at precisely the same time, the rabbis had a problem. This problem of starting the Sabbath throughout the land at the same time could not always be solved by the three early stars because frequently those stars were hidden by clouds.

What were the rabbis to do?

As always, they developed a solution. Should it be that the sunset cannot be observed, they decreed, the Sabbath can be pin-pointed when the fowls settle on their perches to roost.

Across the centuries, the services in the temple became more ritualistic. The original command was extremely simple: "Six days shall work be done: but the seventh day is the sabbath of rest, an holy convocation; ye shall do no work therein: it is the sabbath of the Lord in all your dwellings" (Leviticus 23:3).

That passage and others in Numbers 4:7-14, and 28 were about the only instructions Moses had proclaimed. But on the Sabbath that followed the crucifixion of Jesus, both the morning and evening sacrifices were, as they had been for hundreds of years, a maze of precise dos and don'ts.

The first ceremony that had to be performed was to

renew the showbread—the "Bread of the Presence." Altogether, there were twelve loaves—one for each tribe in Israel. Each loaf was made from approximately five pints of wheat flour that had been shaken through a sieve eleven times. The loaves were arranged in two rows on a table two cubits wide, one cubit broad, and one and a half cubits high. Crafted out of pure gold, its legs were turned outward in the manner of a lamb.

This table had to be placed on the northern side of the Holy Place. Next, two bowls filled with incense were set amidst the loaves of bread. Each loaf was anointed in the middle with dedicated oil carefully shaped in the form of a cross.

The bread had to be the correct size. The specifications, were explicit. Each loaf must be ten handbreadths long and five handbreadths wide. Also, two handbreadths on both sides at the ends had to be curled up. This was so that the loaves, Israel's recognition that God supplied their daily bread, would resemble the Ark of the Covenant.

Showbread was prepared during the week. From the oven it was placed in a golden dish and carefully preserved on a marble-topped table stationed on the porch of the sanctuary.

The bread remained on this table until the morning of the Sabbath. Exchanging the "old" bread for the new bread was a complicated procedure. The Mishnah—a collection of Jewish traditions compiled around A.D. 200—explains how this was done. "Four priests enter [the Holy Place], two carrying . . . the piles of showbread, the other two the two dishes [of incense]. . . . Those who brought in [the bread and incense] stood at the north side [of the table], facing southward. . . . The showbread which had been taken off was then deposited on the golden table in the porch of the sanctuary . . . after which the showbread was distributed among the outgoing and the incoming course of priests. The incoming priests stood at the northside, the outgoing at the southside, and each course gave to the high-priest half of their portion. The showbread was eaten during the Sabbath, and in the Temple itself, but only by such priests as were in a state of Levitical purity" (Edersheim 1950, 185-186).

The officiating priests during each day's services were chosen by lot. New Testament readers will remember the aged and childless priest, Zacharias. He along with others had been chosen by lot to officiate for one week in the temple. Again by chance and for the first time in his life, he was selected to officiate at the burning of incense in the Holy Place. This was the most honorable service that could be performed during the day. (See Luke 1:5-60.)

Due to the ritual, Zacharias' assignment was complex.

On being chosen, he was required to go into another room. There, other priests told him the exact location of the chafing dish. They also informed him that he should not touch this dish or any other sacred vessel until he had washed his hands and feet: "Your right hand will wash your right foot; and your left hand will wash your left foot."

Edersheim relates the account of the ritual:

> While assistant priests waited, the first priest took the silver chafing dish, and scraped the fire on the altar, removing the burnt coals, and depositing them at a slight distance north of the altar. As he descended, other priests quickly washed hands and feet, and took shovels and prongs, with which they moved aside . . . the sacrifices that had been left unburned from the previous evening, then cleaned out the ashes, laying part on the great heap in the middle of

the altar, and the rest in a place where it was afterwards carried out of the Temple. The next duty was to lay on the altar fresh wood, which, however, might be neither from the olive nor the vine. For the fire destined to feed the altar of incense the wood of the fig tree was exclusively used so as to secure good and sufficient charcoal. The hitherto unconsumed pieces of the sacrifice were now again laid on the fire.

These preliminaries finished, the priests gathered once more for the *second* lot (160).

The priest chosen during the second casting was the one who would kill the daily sacrifice. But before he was allowed to do this, the "president" asked another to climb the highest pinnacle and give a report in regard to the position of the sun. If he reported, "The morning sun is already shining," he was asked, "Is the sky lit up as far as Hebron?"

Should the report be "yes," the president ordered that the lamb that had been kept in readiness for four days be brought in. While this was taking place, other priests brought in the gold and silver vessels that were needed. At this point, the sacrificial lamb was watered from a golden bowl and carefully examined to make certain that it was without blemish. Next, the priest who had been selected by lot to kill the lamb, fastened it to the second ring on the north side of the altar. The position of the selected ring depended on whether it was the morning or evening sacrifice. In the morning it was on the western side, in the evening the eastern side. Since the sacrifice had to be offered *against* the sun, the lamb's head was positioned toward the south, and its face directed toward the west. During the morning sacrifice, the sacrificing priest stood on the east side. At the evening sacrifice, these positions were reversed.

When all was ready, the elders in charge of the keys, gave an order to open the gates of the temple. The instant these massive gates, began to creak, the priests with the silver trumpets blew three blasts.

Their blasts alerted other priests to open the massive gates that led to the Holy Place so that those chosen to cleanse the candlestick and the altar of incense could enter. As these gates began to move on their hinges, the one who had been chosen to slay the lamb pushed his knife into its gullet. Its blood was then sprinkled on the altar of burnt-offering.

Following additional ceremonies, the lamb was placed on a hook, skinned, and cut into pieces in accordance with extremely intricate rules. After salting the skin, the most solemn part of the ceremonies began. The incensing priest, along with his assistants, now approached the altar of burnt-offering. One carried a golden censer filled with incense, another carried a golden bowl filled with live coals from off the altar. Upon reaching the Holy Place, the assistant with the live coals reverently spread them onto the golden altar, while the one with the incense positioned the golden incense-container near the coals. Next, the president announced: "The time of incense has come." Responding to his announcement, the entire congregation "fell down before the Lord, spreading their hands in silent prayer." Then, as the vast assembly remained in this position, the appointed priest slowly spread the incense onto the live coals and thus filled the place with a cloud of fragrant odors.

Numerous ritualistic prayers were intoned by the priests.

Following these supplications, another priest selected by lot, tossed the carefully cut sections of the sacrificed lamb onto the glowing coals. As these sections burned, the line of priests on the steps of the altar lifted their hands above their heads and joined their fingers in an especially prescribed way. While immovable in this position, one of them quoted the passage from Numbers 6:24-26: "Jehovah bless thee, and keep thee: Jehovah make his face shine upon thee, and give thee peace."

In answer, the people replied: "Blessed be the Lord God, of Israel, from everlasting to everlasting."

After additional ceremonies, it was time for the morning psalm accompanied by temple music. Each day of the week had assigned to it a particular psalm. The choice never varied. On the first day it was Psalm 24. This psalm had been chosen because the first line, "The earth is the Lord's," honored the first day of creation. Each selection honored the Lord for a special action or attribute.

This morning, being the Sabbath, Mary and John listened as the choir, accompanied by trumpets and the periodic crashing of cymbals, sang the Psalm 92.

Knowing Mary's heart was heavy, it's easy for us to wonder what kind of thoughts presented themselves to her as the Levites sang the fourth verse: "For thou, Lord, hast made me glad through thy work: I will triumph in the works of thy hands."

To Mary, at that moment, God's works with her son had indeed been bitter works. In spite of the cymbals and the trumpets and the many-voiced choir, she could still see and hear him as in utter agony, he cried: "My God, My God, why hast thou forsaken me?" (Mark 15:34). Those and other memories drenched her eyes.

* * *

Back in John's home, Mary did not have sufficient appetite to take even a single bite of the unleavened bread. The word *why* kept flashing in her mind. On many occasions, the statements of Jesus in regard to his coming death had been reiterated to her.

One afternoon, John had carefully repeated her son's words: "Therefore doth my Father love me, because I lay down my life, that I might take it again. No man taketh it from me, but I lay it down of myself. I have power to lay it down, and I have power to take it again. This commandment have I received of my Father" (John 10:17-18).

Facing John, she said, "Don't be annoyed with me for asking the same question again and again. Remember, I'm his mother!"

"I'm not annoyed," John, smiled broadly "Ask any question you like."

Eyes blurred, she said, "Tell me, John, did he *really* say that he would arise on the third day?"

"He did. I distinctly remember when he said to all twelve of us: 'Behold we go up to Jerusalem, and all things that are written by the prophets concerning the Son of man shall be accomplished. For he shall be delivered unto the Gentiles, and shall be mocked, . . . and the *third* day he shall rise again' " (Luke 18:31-33, emphasis added).

* * *

As shadows lengthened, several spent time discussing the temple veil that had been torn from top to bottom at the moment of Jesus' death. (Matt. 27:51; Mark 15:38; and Luke 23:45.)

"Do you think it was done by the earthquake?" asked one.

"Never," replied another. "It was done by the hand of God!"

"What does that mean?" demanded the second man, his jaw sagging.

"I-I don't know," replied the first man. "It won't be long until the Day of Atonement, and I'm worried."

"Why?"

"Why! Because of sin. God created the Day of Atonement so that our sins could be forgiven." He swallowed hard. "That's the only day in the year when the high-priest is allowed to enter the Holy of Holies. But now that the veil is torn, the Holy of Holies can no longer be a secret place." He slapped his cheeks. "I don't know about the rest of you, but I know I'm a sinner. My only access to God is through the high priest!"

"Maybe the veil can be replaced," suggested a bent old man with long hairs flowing from the rims of his ears.

"It could never be repaired in time for the next Day of Atonement which, if you've forgotten, is on the tenth of Tishri" (September-October).

"That's seven months from now," grunted the old man.

"True, but do you know the size of the veil? It's sixty feet tall, thirty feet wide—and as thick as the palm of my hand. It will take time and scores of workers to repair it!"

* * *

Like the Passover, the Day of Atonement—affectionately called The Day—had accumulated many colorful legends since its inauguration (Leviticus 16:23-32, 25:9; and Numbers 29:11). It was considered to be the actual day on which Adam and Eve sinned and repented; the actual day on which Abraham was circumcised; and the actual day on which Moses made atonement for the sins of the Israelites in worshiping the golden calf.

"Seven days before [a] Day of Atonement the high-priest left his own house . . . and took up his abode in the . . . Temple. . . . During the whole of that week . . . he had to practice the various priestly rights. . . . On the eve of the Day . . . the various sacrifices were brought before him, that there might be nothing strange about the services on the morrow. . . .

"The services on [a normal Day of Atonement] began with the first streak of morning light. . . .

"Altogether [the high-priest] changed his raiment and washed his whole body *five* times, and his hands and feet *ten* times . . ." [After changing from his golden vestments, he bathed and put on linen garments and continued on with the ritual].

"The bullock for his sin-offering stood between the Temple porch and the altar. It was placed toward the south, but the high-priest, who stood facing the east [that is, the worshipers], turned the head of the sacrifice toward the west [that is to face the sanctuary]. He then laid both his hands on the bullock, and confessed:

> Ah, Jehovah! I have committed iniquity; I have transgressed; I have sinned—I and my house. Oh, then, Jehovah, I entreat Thee, cover over (atone for, let there be atonement for) the iniquities, the transgressions, and the sins which I have committed, transgressed and sinned before Thee, I and my house—even as it is written in the law of Moses, Thy servant: "For on that day will he cover over (atone) for you to make you clean; from all your transgressions before Jehovah ye shall be cleansed" (307-310).

* * *

Following an additional ritual in which the high-priest used the word Jehovah ten times, and the people responded: "Blessed be the Name; the glory of His kingdom is for ever and ever," two identical goats, chosen by lot, were led to a place before the high priest. The high priest then tied a scarlet tongue of cloth on the horn of the animal had been chosen as the "scapegoat." Then he tied a similar cloth around the throat of the second animal designated to represent Jehovah. Edersheim continues,

> The [scape-goat] was now turned . . . toward the people, and stood facing them, waiting . . . till their sins be laid upon him, and he would carry them forth to 'a land not inhabited.'
> Then, the high-priest killed the bullock. . . . Advancing toward the altar of burnt-offering, he . . . filled the censer with burning coals, and then arranged a handful of incense in the right and the censer in the left. . . . Every eye . . . strained toward the sanctuary as, slowly bearing the censer and the incense the figure of the white-robed high-priest was seen to disappear into the Holy Place. After that nothing could be seen of his movements.
> The curtain of the Holy Place was folded back, and the high-priest stood alone and separated from all the people in the awful gloom of the Holiest of All, only lit up by the red coals in the priest's censer. . . .
> While the incense was offering in the Most Holy Place the people . . . worshiped in silence. . . . [When they saw] the high-priest emerging from the sanctuary . . . they knew that the service had been accepted" (312-315).

The involved ritual continued as the listeners followed in a most solemn manner. Eventually the high priest emerged from the Most Holy Place. Then he killed the goat designated to represent Jehovah, and returned to the Most Holy Place. Again he sprinkled blood:

> Finally pouring the blood of the bullock into the bowl which contained the blood of the goat . . . he thoroughly commingled the two. [Next] he sprinkled each of the horns of the

altar of incense, and then, making a clear place on the altar. . . . [Eventually] he had sprinkled forty-three times with the expiatory blood, taking care that his own dress should never be spotted with the sin-laden blood. . . .

[Finally] the priests led the sin-burdened goat through Solomon's Porch, and, as tradition has it, through the Eastern Gate which opened upon the Mount of Olives. Here an arched bridge spanned the intervening valley, and over it they brought the goat to the Mount of Olives, where one specially appointed for the purpose took him in charge. Tradition enjoins that he should be a stranger, a non-Israelite. . . . At last they reached the edge of the wilderness. Here they halted . . . while the man who led forward the goat, tore off half the "scarlet-tongue,' and stuck it on a projecting cliff; then leading the animal backwards, he pushed it over the projecting edge of the rock" (318-319).

News that the sin-bearing goat was now in the wilderness was rushed to Jerusalem by flag-relays. When it reached the temple there was ecstatic rejoicing. The news meant that all the sins that Israel had committed during the year had been carried away by the scapegoat into the wilderness and had been forgiven!

* * *

Exhausted from the excitement, Mary did not attend the Evening Sacrifice. Eyes on the sun as it neared the horizon, she followed the glowing disk anxiously as it continued to sink. The instant it sank beyond the horizon, the First Day of the new week would be upon them. Its arrival would mean that Jesus had been in the tomb for at least a portion of three days.

Jesus had assured the Twelve that he would be resurrected on the third day. . . . *But were his words to be taken literally?*

Suddenly as the sun disappeared Mary heard the haunting sound of a ram's horn. Did the announcement that the Sabbath had ended mean that the world was facing a new era? Her mind in a whirl, Mary bowed her head and prayed.

* * *

Can You Answer?

1. How did the rabbis determine the arrival of a new day?
2. Across the centuries, did the temple services change?
3. How many loaves of showbread were displayed?
4. Out of what was the showbread made?
5. What was the purpose of showbread?
6. Which psalm was sung in the temple on the Sabbath? On the First Day?
7. What was the main purpose of the scapegoat?
8. How was the scapegoat pushed over the cliff?

8 Easter Morning

Inspired by the Holy Spirit and gripped by God's assignment, the authors of the gospels became great writers—and they wrote in such a way that readers would be inspired by the action and message rather than by their words or style of writing. Since they wrote under God's command, they, like Moses in the first chapter of Genesis, merely touched the highlights.

In that this was the way it was meant to be, if we want a three-dimensional picture of Easter morning, we must look at all four of the Gospels—and read between the lines. For example, where was Mary on that era-closing and era-opening day? All we know is that as Jesus was dying on the cross, he assigned John the task of caring for his mother; we are told that "From that hour that disciple took her into his own home" (John 19:27). The fact is apparent therefore that as the fifteenth of Nisan faded, and the sixteenth of Nisan was born, Mary was in the beloved disciple's home.

With this as an explanation, we will proceed.

While Mary sat before a tiny lamp, her ears were alert for any unexpected sound. As Jesus was growing up, Mary had become accustomed to the crunch of his feet and his knock at the door. But as she listened, all she heard was the swish of the wind, the moaning of the trees, the chirp and buzz of insects, and the distant bark of a dog from beyond the Eastern Gate.

Eyelids heavy, Mary's mind wandered back to the occasion when she and her husband took Jesus to Jerusalem at the age of twelve. Losing him in the throngs, she and Joseph returned to the place where they had last seen him. There, they found him discussing weighty matters with the doctors in the temple. Thoroughly annoyed, for he'd been out of their sight for three days, Mary had chided him. Now, as she rehearsed the incident, she remembered both what she had said and his reply.

"Son," she had admonished, "why hast thou thus treated with us? Behold thy father and I have sought thee sorrowing."

His reply was terse: "How is it that ye sought me? Wist ye not that I must be about my Father's business?" (Luke 2:48-49).

As a smile at the memory turned up her lips, Mary reasoned: *Jesus knows what he's doing; why should I be anxious when he's fulfilling God's plan for humankind?* With that thought comforting her heart, she returned to her room and tried to sleep.

After rolling and tossing and changing positions, she finally dozed off. Then suddenly she was awakened by a loud thumping at the door. Startled, she slapped on her clothes and rushed downstairs. There, standing before her was Peter exchanging greetings with John.

"Oh, I thought it was Jesus!" she exclaimed. Before Peter could answer, she asked, "Have you seen him?"

"No, I haven't."

"Have any of the other disciples seen him?"

"Not that I know of—"

"But this is the *third* day!" Mary's voice was tense.

"True. B-but m-maybe Jesus just meant for us to take his teachings seriously. He was constantly speaking in parables."

"Then, where is he?" Mary tightened her gown.

"I-I d-don't know. His body is probably still in the tomb."

After a long pause, John said, "You are welcome to stay with us. But why did you come so late?"

"I was visiting with friends, and I had to wait until after sunset because it's more than a Sabbath's journey from where I was staying on the south side of Jerusalem."

"Had any of those you met on the way seen Jesus?"

"No. Several women said that it was a pity that Jesus had been crucified, but that his words would continue to live," Peter shrugged.

"We're glad that you came," broke in John, taking him by the hand. "But you need to rest. Let me take you to one of our extra beds." He laughed. Then smiling at Mary, he added: "We fishermen have learned to get along with one another!"

* * *

Long before daylight, Mary Magdalene, Mary the mother of James—and Salome, perhaps the wife of Zebedee (Matt. 27:56) or a sister of Mary the mother of Jesus (John 19:25), got together. They met to complete their selection of spices to place in the shroud of Jesus in the tomb provided by Joseph of Arimathea.

All these women knew exactly where the tomb was located, for they had lingered at the crucifixion and had watched as Joseph and Nicodemus prepared Jesus' body, placed it in the tomb, and closed it with a huge circular stone. (See John 19:25; Matt. 27:61; and Mark 15:47. These passages do not mention Salome, but she may have been one of the women mentioned in Luke 23:55.)

After agreeing that they had sufficient spices, they stepped out of their meeting place and headed for the tomb.

* * *

Here we are confronted with a web of apparent discrepancies in the gospels. These discrepancies, the majority of which are trivial, have upset many. Rudolph Bultman declared, "A historical fact which involves a resurrection from the dead is utterly inconceivable" (Zarley 1987, 382).

In contrast to form-critic Bultman, H. A. W. Meyer, a firm believer in the resurrection, candidly wrote:

> In no section of evangelical Christianity have harmonists, with their artificial mosaic work, been compelled to spend more labor, and with less success, than in the section on the resurrection. The adjustment between John and the synoptics, as also between the latter among themselves, is impossible, but the grand fact itself and the chief traits of history stand all the more firmly (381).

* * *

Weighted with spices, "Mary Magdalene, and Mary the mother of James, and Salome" (Mark 16:1), continued on their mission to honor the remains of their friend.

Here Mark's story is faced with a difficulty.

Problem. Mark mentioned the three women who were engaged in this procedure. But Matthew only mentioned two—"Mary Magdalene and the other Mary" (28:1). Moreover, he didn't say a word about spices; but rather that they went "to *see* the sepulchre." In contrast, Luke didn't name any of the women. He merely referred to them as *they*. But the antecedent of *they* is in verse 55. It refers to the "women . . . also, which came from Galilee" (23:55 and 24:1). Unlike the above three, John merely mentioned Mary Magdalene (20:1).

Solution. The fact is that the number of women mentioned means nothing. The detail that John only mentioned Mary Magdalene does not imply that there were no other women present. Also, a reasonable assumption is that no woman would want to be alone, especially at that time in the morning. Likewise, the fact that all the gospel writers did not mention spices does not mean that there were no spices.

A Jewish custom was to visit the grave of the departed on the third day after burial. This custom may have seemed more important to Matthew and John. Also, remember that Matthew recorded that "Mary Magdalene and the other Mary" were at the sepulcher when Joseph and Nicodemus prepared the body.

* * *

Mark 16:1-4 informs us (A) "that the women came unto the sepulchre at the *rising of the sun*" (emphasis added); (B) that they were concerned about who would roll away the stone "from the door of the sepulchre"; (C) without the explanation of an angel or an earthquake "the stone was rolled away."

Problem. (A) Disagreeing with Mark, John wrote: "it was yet dark when they reached the sepulchre" (20:1). Luke's version is slightly different. He used the words:

"early in the morning." Bookkeeper Matthew, however, probably solved the difficulty. According to him: *"as it began to dawn toward the first day of the week,* came Mary Magdalene and the other Mary to see the sepulchre" (28:1, emphasis added).

Solution. Matthew's in-between version may be the key. Researchers, however, have proposed various answers to this problem of time. Among them is the proposal that the women visited on the way. This solution is unacceptable, for the simple reason that they were burdened with spices.

* * *

Problem. This one concerns the stone. Matthew wrote: "Behold, there was a great earthquake: for the angel of the Lord descended from heaven, and came and rolled back the stone from the door and sat upon it" (28:2). Mark's comment is simply "When they looked, they saw that the stone was rolled away" (16:4). Luke ignored the problem of the stone by saying: "They found the stone rolled away from the sepulchre" (24:2).

Again this seemed no problem to John. He ignored it!

Solution. Kermit Zarley may have solved the puzzle by outlining the events that had taken place within a few minutes on that Sunday morning. His scenario:

a. There was a violent earthquake (Matt. 28:2).
b. An angel came down from heaven and rolled back the stone and sat on it (v. 2).
c. The guards saw him, shook, and fainted (vv. 2-4).
d. The guards awoke and went to tell the authorities. (v. 11).

* * *

Problem. A question asked by many concerns the spices. Why would the women want to add spices to the remains when Joseph of Arimathea and Nicodemus had already prepared them with ample cloth and one hundred pounds of spices? At this point, Ahmed Deedat in his *Crucifixion or Cruci-fiction* is caustic:

> The question arises: Why did she [Mary Magdalene] go there? 'To *anoint him*' Mark tells us. The Hebrew word for anoint is *masha*, which means to rub, to massage, to anoint. The second question is: Do Jews massage dead bodies after three days? The answer is *No!* . . . Then why would a Jewess want to massage a dead, decaying body, after three days? We know that within three hours rigor mortis sets in. . . . In three days time the body would be fermenting within. . . . If anyone rubs such a decaying body, it will fall to pieces. Does rubbing make sense? No! (Deedat 1984, 44).

Solution. Many words have several meanings. It is therefore a violation of common sense to apply only one meaning to all situations. The word *anoint* is found all through the Bible. In Exodus 29 this word is used in several ways: "Then thou shalt take the anointing oil and *pour* it upon his head, and anoint him" (v. 7, emphasis added). "Thou shalt take of the blood that is upon the altar, and of the anointing oil, and *sprinkle* it upon Aaron (v. 21, emphasis added). "Thou shalt offer every day a bullock *for* a sin offering for atonement . . . and thou shalt *anoint* it to sanctify it" (v. 36, emphasis added).

Remember that Jesus had only been in the tomb for a fragment of three days. The one full day in *daylight* hours—presumably warm hours—was Saturday. In addition, parts of the morning daylight hours were cool. The records indicate that on Friday Jesus had worn a robe, and Simon Peter had warmed himself at a fire.

But why would they want to anoint the body? Some have reasoned that one motivation was to show their respect and another was to help preserve the body.

* * *

Having found that the stone had been rolled away, Mark wrote that the women entered the sepulcher (16:5) and Luke concurs (24:3). But Matthew merely indicated that an angel *invited* them to enter the sepulcher. "Come, see the place where the Lord lay" (28:6). But he does not say that they entered! John, however, skipped this part of the story completely.

Problem. In addition to the fact that only Mark and Luke mention that the women actually entered the sepulcher, there is the problem of the angels. That problem includes their number, their positions at the tomb—and their appearance.

Matthew spoke of only *one* angel whom he describes as being "like lightning" and whose raiment was "white as snow." He did not indicate the way the angel was positioned (28:2-6).

Like Matthew, Mark mentioned only one angel; but he referred to him as "a young man." In contrast, Mark stationed him *inside* the sepulcher. Nonetheless, his description of the "being's" raiment parallels that of Matthew (Mark 16:5).

Luke and John's number of "angels" differ from Mark "as they were much perplexed thereabout, behold *two* men stood by them in shining garments" (Luke 24:4; John 20:12).

At this time—during Mary Magdalene's *first* visit—John did not mention angels!

Ah, but we're concerned about the position of the angels.

Mark says that they saw "a young man *sitting* on the

right side" (v. 5). But Luke says "behold two men *stood* by them in shining garments" (24:4).

Solution. The differences in the accounts by the gospel writers is not as pronounced as might appear. Luke and John agree that there were two angels. (See John's account about Mary Magdalene's *second* visit, 20:11-12.) A possibility is that Matthew and Mark referred to only one angel because one angel was the spokesperson. But did the angel or angels stand or sit? Probably they both stood *and* sat!

The fact that both Luke and Matthew referred to these brightly clothed beings as "men" is no contradiction, for angels often appeared as men. (Combine Genesis 18:2 with 19:1.)

* * *

Upon entering the tomb (Mark 16:5 and Luke 24:3) the women were addressed by an angel. At this point we turn to John 20:1-2. In that passage, John only mentioned that Mary Magdalene had been to the tomb. But he does not say that she entered. Instead, he merely commented that she went *"unto* the sepulchre."

Now we come to the angel's instructions. Matthew recorded that he said, "Go quickly and tell his disciples that he is risen from the dead; and behold, he goeth before you into Galilee; there shall ye see him" (28:7). Mark also wrote that he said that Jesus would proceed before them to Galilee. In addition, he instructed that they should mention his resurrection to Peter." Luke merely noted that the angel had said, "He is not here, but is risen." But he did not record that the angel had assigned them the duty to go and tell anyone (24:6-10).

John's report did not allude to any angelic instructions. He only stated that Mary Magdalene had been to the tomb (20:1).

Now we come to the exciting drama that took place immediately *after* the women had been to the burial place. Again we have a variety of reports: Matthew: "They departed quickly from the sepulchre with fear and great joy; *and did run to bring his disciples word*" (28:8, emphasis added). Mark: "They went out quickly, and fled from the sepulchre; for they trembled and were amazed: *neither said they any thing to any man; for they were afraid*" (16:8, emphasis added).

Luke did not mention an angelic assignment. Nonetheless, he wrote: "They remembered his [Jesus'] words, And returned from the sepulchre, *and told all these things unto the eleven, and to all the rest.* It was Mary Magdalene, and Joanna, and Mary the mother of James, and other women that were with them, which told these things unto the apostles. And their words seemed to them as idle tales, and they believed them not" (24:8-11). What did John say? "Then she [Mary Magdalene] runneth, and cometh to Simon Peter, and to the other disciple, whom Jesus loved, and saith unto them, *They have taken away the Lord, out of the sepulchre, and we know not where they have laid him*" (20:2).

* * *

Problem. Here we are faced with a cluster of obstacles that could almost be referred to as conundrums. Matthew declared that they "[ran] to bring his disciples *word.*" But reliable Mark commented: "*neither said they anything to any man.*" On the other hand Luke reported that they: "*told all these things to the eleven and to all the rest*" (24:9, emphasis added).

John, an eyewitness, and one who was involved, was categorical: Mary Magdalene had returned from the tomb and had reported the news to both him and Simon Peter.

With these apparent contradictions, a non-believing attorney could have a good time as he summed up his case before a jury. One could imagine a rotund man snapping his suspenders, shaking his finger and shouting: "This is an open-and-shut case. Not only were these words of Matthew, Mark, Luke, and John written from twenty-five to sixty years after the event, but they are crowded with blatant discrepancies and contradictions.

"Who are we to believe—Matthew, Mark, Luke, or John? As for me, I don't believe any of them! Bultman is correct. Jesus Christ was never resurrected from the dead."

Solution. Since Kermit Zarley spent years mulling over this problem and consulting with scholars, we will quote at length from his *The Gospels Interwoven*:

> All three synoptists appear to indicate that on her first visit to the tomb . . . Mary Magdalene entered with the other women, saw the angel(s) and heard their announcement that Jesus was risen (cf. Matt. 28:1 with vv. 5-7 and Mark 16:1 with vv. 5-7; cf. Luke 24:10 with vv. 3-7).
>
> Luke relates that Mary Magdalene and the other women returned and *told all these things to the eleven and to all the others . . . but they did not believe the women* (Luke 24:10-11). Yet John quotes Mary Magdalene as first telling Peter and himself, *"They have taken the Lord out of the tomb, and we don't know where they have put him"* (John 20:2, NIV, emphasis added), as if she had never heard the angels' announcement. It is possible that Mary Magdalene failed to believe the announcement. . . . Perhaps this is indicated by the report of the two returning from Emmaus.
>
> They recounted that the women *had seen a vision of angels* (Luke 24:23). This may indicate that the women, including Mary Magdalene,

were uncertain whether their experience was a vision or an actual angel encounter, as the synoptists clearly present. If so, this suggests that they too were slow to believe what the angels had announced" (Zarley 391).

(The experience of realizing that their master had risen from the dead, seeing angels in shining clothes, and hearing them speak, was not only awe-inspiring, it was breathtaking! It reminds one of the time Luther stood before Charles V. Although facing death, he had the sublime courage to declare: "Here I stand. I cannot do otherwise. God help me. Amen." Great words. And yet the shorthand reporters failed to record the angel's words. Why? They were overwhelmed!.)

Zarley notes:

Some expositors presume that upon initially seeing the removed tombstone, and before entering the tomb, the women discussed among themselves which one of them should run and tell Peter and John, and that Mary Magdalene was chosen because of her youth. But this is only conjecture" (391).

* * *

Mary Magdalene was panting when she confronted Peter and John with the news that Jesus had risen from the dead. John recorded: "Then she runneth and cometh to Simon Peter, and to the other disciple whom Jesus loved, and saith unto them, They have taken away the Lord from out the sepulchre, and we know not where they have laid him" (20:2).

Peter and John took off immediately. As they ran, John outran Peter. But although John reached the sepulcher first, he waited for Peter to come puffing up before entering. In the meantime he stooped and "looking in, saw the linen clothes lying" (John 20:5). At that moment he might have reasoned: *I was with Peter when he went to sleep in the garden, and hacked off a man's ear. And I was with him when he cursed and denied that he had ever known Jesus outside the hall of Caiaphas. Therefore I should have the honor to be the first one to enter the tomb.*

But just as John had been polite enough not to call Peter's attention his denial as they ran, he allowed Peter to be the first to enter. Why? Perhaps it was because he was dazed with awe; or perhaps it was because he remembered how Jesus had washed their feet in the Upper Room.

Even so, John had the much greater honor by being the only one to record: "[Peter] went into the sepulchre, and seeth the linen clothes lie, And the napkin, that was about his head, not lying with the linen clothes, but wrapped together in a place by itself" (John 20:6-7) and then to add, "Then went in also that other disciple, which came first to the sepulchre, and he saw, and believed" (v. 8). Thus we have his own testimony that he was the first one to accept the fact of the resurrection!

* * *

So far we've reviewed the visit to the tomb and the message of the angels. But to whom did the resurrected Christ first appear? Again we're faced with conflict. We'll analyze that conundrum, and evaluate the appearances, in the next chapter.

Can You Answer?

1. What was Jesus doing when he was "lost" in the temple?
2. Why did the women visit the tomb?
3. How many women were they? What were their names?
4. Since it was partially dark, how did the women find their way?
5. How can we reconcile the fact that Matthew and Mark only referred to one angel, while Luke said there were two?
6. Who reached the tomb first, Peter or John?
7. Which disciple was the first to believe in the resurrected Christ?

9 Those World-Changing Appearances

The appearances of the resurrected Christ changed the world! Even so, careful Bible students realize that the records of his appearances are splattered with difficulties.

To whom did Jesus first appear? Was it Peter as apparently affirmed by both Luke and Paul? (See Luke 24:33-34; 1 Cor. 15:5.) Or did he first appear to Mary Magdalene as emphatically stated by Mark: "He appeared *first* to Mary Magdalene, out of whom he had cast seven devils" (16:9, emphasis added), a conviction also assumed by John: "[Mary Magdalene] turned herself back, and saw Jesus standing, and knew not that it was Jesus?" (20:14).

Also, why did the angel instruct the women to "tell his disciples and Peter that he goeth before you into *Galilee*?" (Mark 16:7, emphasis added). This raises eyebrows, because Jesus appeared to the Eleven that Sunday evening in *Jerusalem*, a fact that is also stated by two other writers: Luke 24:33-36 and John 20:19.

This is complicated even more by Matthew who testified that Jesus appeared to the Eleven in *Galilee*, at "a mountain where he [Jesus] had *appointed* them" (28:16-17, emphasis added). Likewise, Matthew mentioned only one appearance in Jerusalem! This was the appearance to the women (28:9).

Solution. Let's begin by deciding to whom Jesus appeared first. Curiously, Paul did not say categorically that Jesus appeared *first* to Peter. He merely stated that "he was seen of Cephas, then of the twelve" (1 Cor. 15:5). Likewise, neither did Luke say that he appeared first to Peter. Rather, Luke quoted one who had seen him on the road to Emmaus as saying: "The Lord is risen indeed, and hath appeared to Simon" (24:34).

Also, Matthew did not claim that the mountain appearance was the *first* appearance. But the fact that this assertion is right after he related the way the guards at the tomb had been bribed to lie to the authorities by saying, "His disciples came by night, and stole him away while we slept" (28:13), suggests that Matthew was indicating that this was the *first* appearance.

Even so, what do we do with Mark's remark that Jesus appeared first to Mary Magdalene (16:9), and Matthew's statement when he quoted the angel at the tomb as saying, "Go quickly and tell his disciples that he is risen from the dead; . . . and [the women] departed quickly from the sepulchre with fear and great joy; and did run to bring his disciples word. . . . And as they went to tell his disciples, behold, *Jesus met them, saying All hail. And they came and held him by the feet?*" (28:7-9, emphasis added).

Another part of this problem—a major part—is whether Mary Magdalene or the "women" who were on their way to tell the Good News to the disciples were first to see the risen Christ. This difficulty is compounded by the fact that Matthew assured us that Mary Magdalene was among the women who had been at the tomb (28:1).

This obstacle has been unraveled by Kermit Zarley. After referring to the statement by Matthew, Zarley continues:

> But Luke 24:9 reads: *When they came back from the tomb, they told all these things to the Eleven* (NIV, emphasis added), indicating that the women first told the disciples only of the empty tomb and the angel's announcement (vv. 4-8), not that they had seen the Lord Jesus. This is further corroborated by the two disciples walking to Emmaus, when they told Jesus, that *Some of our women amazed us. They went to the tomb early this morning but didn't find his body. They came and told us that they had seen a vision of angels, who said he was alive* (Luke 24:22-23, NIV, emphasis added). Here is conclusive evidence that the women did not see Jesus until after they first reported the empty tomb to the disciples. Luke includes Mary Magdalene among the women who told the disciples of the empty tomb (v. 10). If Jesus had already appeared to her with the other women, Mary's failure to recognize him at the later appearance alone that day (John 20:10-18) would be inexplicable.
>
> Therefore, it is certain that a time gap exists between Matthew 28:8 and 9 into which are inserted certain events recorded in the other gospels. (Zarley 394-395).

Zarley suggests the following time schedule. Here it is in my own words:

a. The women saw that the stone had been removed and they looked inside the tomb (Matt. 28:1; Luke 24:3).
b. Mary Magdalene rushed by herself to inform Peter and John that the tomb was empty. She may not have gone inside and heard the command of the angels (John 20:1-2). Or, perhaps she entered, heard the angels, but was so flabbergasted by their appearance that their message didn't register.
c. The other women, then, by themselves, entered the tomb, met the angels, and heard one of them say that Jesus had been resurrected (Matt. 28:5-7; Mark 16:5-7; Luke 24:4-7).
d. The women hurried to relay the news to the disciples.
e. Mary Magdalene reached John's house first and announced "They have taken away the Lord . . . and we know not where they have laid him!" she exclaimed (John 20:2).
f. Peter and John ran the entire distance to the tomb.
g. Mary Magdalene *returned* to the tomb. On her return Jesus made his *first* appearance (Mark 16:9; John 20:11-16.)

* * *

We're now confronted with another problem. Before his crucifixion Jesus had said, "But after I am risen again, I will go before you into Galilee" (Matt. 26:32). Then, *after* his resurrection, he sent word to the disciples by an angel, through the women, that they should "go into Galilee" with the promise that "there shall they see me" (Matt. 28:10). This same command is in Mark 16:7. Since Jesus had personally told the Eleven that he would meet *them* in Galilee, and through an angel that he would meet the *disciples* in Galilee, why were his first appearances in Jerusalem? This problem has puzzled scholars for centuries.

One guess is that Jesus did not intend for the Eleven to leave Jerusalem immediately for Galilee. After all, they were in the midst of the Feast of Unleavened Bread; and as pious Jews, to leave the feast before it was concluded would be abhorrent. In addition, Galilee was approximately sixty miles north of Jerusalem—a journey of two or three days. Also, Jesus did not tell the Eleven *when* he would meet them in Galilee.

Another guess is that when the angels spoke to the women, their message was: "*Tell the disciples that I go before them into Galilee,*" emphasis added. The word *disciples*, like the word *brethren* (Matt. 28:10), did not necessarily mean the *Eleven*. It may have referred to a larger group of believers. This possibility is enhanced by Luke who reported that the angels had instructed them to relay this news to "the eleven, *and to all the rest*" (Luke 24:9, emphasis added).

John is the only one who indicated that Jesus appeared to followers *both* in Galilee (21:1-23) and in Jerusalem (20:14).

Still another surmise is that the word *Galilee* was used in a theological sense—that it was a hint that the Eleven were to evangelize the Gentiles. Isaiah had prophesied, "In the future he will honor Galilee of the Gentiles, by the way of the sea, along the Jordan" (9:1, NIV).

Galilee had been the scene of much of Jesus' activities: his miracles, his sermons, and his calling of the Twelve. Furthermore, it was the native land of the Eleven. (Judas was from Kerioth in the southern part of Judea.) Likewise, as we shall see, he had an extremely important message he had planned to deliver to the Eleven in Galilee. By delivering it in Galilee, backgrounded by the scenes of his early ministry, it would be most effective.

In addition, his appearance in Galilee would return to the fold many who had followed for a time and then drifted away.

Without referring to the reactions of those to whom he had appeared, we will list his appearances in chronological order, starting with the first appearance.

* * *

Jesus appeared to
1. Mary Magdalene on her *second* visit to the tomb early on Sunday morning (Mark 16:9-11; John 20:11-18).
2. The *other* women who held his feet later on Sunday morning (Matthew 28:7-10).
3. Simon Peter on Sunday (Luke 24:34; 1 Corinthians 15:5).
4. The travelers on the way to Emmaus at midday on Sunday (Luke 24:13-32).
5. The ten in the Upper Room on Sunday evening (Mark 16:13; Luke 24:36-49; John 20:19-25).
6. The Eleven in the Upper Room one week later (John 20:26-31; 1 Corinthians 15:5).
7. Seven of the Twelve on Lake Galilee (John 21:1-23).
8. The Eleven on a mountain in Galilee (Matthew 28:16-20; Mark 16:15-18).
9. More than 500, date unknown (1 Corinthians 15:6).
10. James (brother of John), probably in Jerusalem, date unknown (Acts 12:2).

* * *

In chapter 10 we will refer to the appearances and the reaction of those to whom he appeared.

Can You Answer?

1. On which of her visits to the Tomb did Mary Magdalene see Jesus?
2. Did she recognize him? If not, why not?
3. Since the angels instructed the women to tell the disciples that Jesus would go before them into Galilee, why did he appear to the ten and Eleven for the first time in Jerusalem?
4. Who was the first to inform Peter and John that the stone had been rolled away?
5. Did Jesus personally instruct the Eleven that he would meet them in Galilee?
6. How did Peter and John go to the tomb?
7. Which one entered the tomb first, Peter or John? Why?

10 They Met the Resurrected Christ

The appearances of the Resurrected Christ on Easter morning, and later, were crowded with startling drama that included blatant unbelief—even by the Eleven.

If, therefore, we want to have an in-depth picture of those era-shattering appearances, we must consider the reaction of those who witnessed his appearances and that of Jesus *after* his appearance. We will do this in chronological order.

* * *

First appearance. After Mary Magdalene had reported to Peter and John, "They have taken away the Lord out of the sepulchre, and we know not where they have laid him" (John 20:2). Peter and John ran all the way to the tomb (vv. 3-4).

Then Mary Magdalene returned to the tomb on her own. This visit was her *third* one, the first being when she along with friends watched Joseph of Arimathea and Nicodemus prepare the body. (It was on this trip that she met the gardener.) The second trip was at dawn when she and others loaded with spices made their way at the tomb early on Sunday morning.

On this third trip, while convulsed with tears, Mary boldly entered the tomb. Almost instantly she was staggered by seeing "two angels in white sitting, one at the head, and the other at the feet, where the body of Jesus had lain" (John 20:12).

When the angels asked her why she was weeping, she replied: "Because they have taken away my Lord, and I know not where they have laid him" (v. 13).

Mary then "turned herself back" and saw a man she assumed to be the gardener. "Sir," she said, "if you have borne him hence, tell me where thou hast laid him, and I will take him away" (v. 15).

In reply, the man said, "Mary" (v. 16).

Mary was overwhelmed, for she recognized Jesus' voice. Its vibrant tones mixed with authority and love were perfectly the same as they had been when he cast the seven devils out of her. Eyes wide, heart beating wildly, "she turned toward him and cried out in Aramaic, 'Rabboni!' which means teacher" (v. 16).

Dazzled, Mary, must have held out her arms, for Jesus replied: "Do not hold on to me, for I have not yet returned to the Father. Go instead to my brothers and tell them, 'I am returning to my Father and your Father, to my God and your God'" (v. 17, NIV).

This *first* appearance of the resurrected Jesus, at least on earth, proves that Mary had *not* seen him after his resurrection on a *prior* occasion; for, had she seen him on a prior occasion, she would have recognized him in his resurrected body!

Also, Jesus' statement that he had "not yet returned to the Father" underlines the belief that immediately after his death on the cross Jesus fulfilled his promise to the thief that "Today shalt thou be with me in paradise" (Luke 23:43). See chapter 3.

Mary's reaction? Without being commanded either by Jesus or an angel, Mary hurried to spread the Good News (John 20:18).

* * *

The second appearance. This appearance occurred later on Sunday morning *after* Jesus had appeared to Mary at the tomb. *After* the women had been to the tomb and an angel had instructed them to "go quickly, and tell his disciples that he had risen from the dead" (Matt. 28:7), they sped away to fulfill their assignment. As they hurried, "Jesus met them, saying, All Hail" (v. 9).

The women's reaction? "They came and held him by the feet, and worshipped him" (v. 9).

The fact that Jesus told Mary Magdalene not to hold him, and yet allowed the women to hold his feet, is an imponderable no one has satisfactorily explained.

* * *

The third appearance. This appearance was to Peter later on Sunday morning. Curiously, we don't know any details. All we know is derived from the statements of Paul (1 Cor. 15:5) and that of the travelers on the way to Emmaus (Luke 24:34).

* * *

The fourth appearance. This appearance is favored by expositors, for it brims with action—and mystery. In violation of dramatic writing, Luke only named two of its characters involved: Jesus and Cleopas. Cleopas is an unknown who was never mentioned before or after in the entire New Testament. Also, he did not pinpoint the location of Emmaus. His only description of the village is that it was "about threescore furlongs" (seven miles) from Jerusalem (Luke 24:13).

Emmaus was such an obscure hamlet that modern researchers have been unable to place it on a map.

But in spite of not revealing the names of both wayfarers, Luke was so gripped by the implications of this fourth appearance during which Jesus ate bread that he lavished twenty-two verses in recording it.

This is significant, for both Matthew and John ignored it, and Mark merely gave it a glancing referral—"Afterward Jesus appeared in a different form to two of them while they were walking in the country. These returned and reported it to the rest; but they did not believe them either" (16:12-13).

Luke's record, 24:13-33, is one of the most influential documents ever written. While strolling toward Emmaus, Cleopas together with an unnamed friend were discussing the events of the day. As they sauntered along, Jesus mysteriously appeared and accompanied them. But, as Luke explained, "they were kept from recognizing him" (v. 15, NIV).

Joining their conversation, Jesus asked: "What manner of communications are these that ye have with one another, as ye walk, and are sad?" (v. 17).

Cleopas then explained how Jesus, "a prophet mighty in deed and word before God and all the people" (v. 19-20) had been crucified. He also explained the way "certain of them which were with us went to the sepulchre" (v. 24) and discovered that his body was missing.

After patiently listening, Jesus exclaimed, "How foolish you are, and how slow of heart to believe all that the prophets had spoken! Did not the Christ have to suffer these things and then enter his glory?" (vv. 25-26). In this manner, Jesus continued, "And beginning with Moses and all the Prophets, he explained to them what was said in all the Scriptures concerning himself" (v. 27, NIV).

By this time, the evening shadows were lengthening, and so Cleopas and his companion invited this stranger whom they did not recognize to stay with them.

Suddenly the scene changed. The NIV explains: "When he was at the table with them, he took bread, gave thanks, broke it and began to give it to them. Then their eyes were opened and they recognized him, and he disappeared from their sight" (v. 30).

Ecstatically amazed, one of the two exclaimed to the other, "Were not our hearts burning within us while he talked to us on the road and opened the Scriptures to us?" (v. 52).

The travelers' reaction. Again, without being asked to relay the news either by Jesus or an angel, the two hurried back to Jerusalem. Since Emmaus was seven miles away, the trip must have taken nearly two hours. The stars were out when they arrived.

There they discovered that the Eleven, in addition to others, had assembled together. Facing them, the travelers all but shouted, "The Lord is risen indeed, and hath appeared to Simon" (v. 34). Then while those in the room gaped in amazement, they related how Jesus had revealed himself to them when he broke bread, shared it, and began to eat.

* * *

The fifth appearance. While the men from Emmaus were relating their experiences to those in the room,

Jesus mysteriously appeared and greeted them: "Peace be unto you" (v. 36). But instead of returning the greeting, the group sat frozen in silence.

Luke described their reaction in verse 37: "But they were startled and frightened, thinking they saw a ghost. [Jesus] said to them, 'Why are you troubled, and why do doubts rise in your minds? Look at my hands and feet. It is I myself! Touch me and see; a ghost does not have flesh and bones, as you see I have.' When he had said this, he showed them his hands and feet. And while they still did not believe it because of joy and amazement, he asked them, 'Do you have anything here to eat?' They gave him a piece of broiled fish, and he took it and ate it in their presence" (vv. 38-43, NIV).

At this juncture, John added an extremely significant drama that is not mentioned by Matthew, Mark, or Luke. After Jesus had said to them, "Peace be unto you!" he added: "As my Father hath sent me, even so send I you. And when he had said this he breathed on them, and saith unto them, 'Receive ye the Holy Ghost: Whosesoever sins ye remit, they are remitted unto them; and whosesoever sins ye retain, they are retained" (20:21-23).

"The verb used here (*emphysaō*) is that used in the LXX [Septuagint] of Genesis 2:7 where, after fashioning the first human being from dust, God 'breathed into his face the breath of life, and the man became a living soul,' " wrote F. F. Bruce.

In explaining Jesus' meaning when he said: "Whosesoever sins ye remit; they are remitted unto them; and whosesoever sins ye retain, they are retained," Bruce continued: "The two passives—'they are remitted' and 'they are retained'—imply divine agency: the preachers' role is declaratory, but it is God who effectively remits or retains" (Bruce 1983, 392).

The reaction of the Ten. Thomas was missing (John

20:24). Luke does not use words to tell how the ten reacted other than to say "he opened their minds so they could understand the Scriptures" (24:45, NIV). But they apparently believed, for he commissioned them to remain in Jerusalem until they would be "endued with power from on high" (v. 49).

* * *

The sixth appearance. This appearance John tells us was "after eight days again"—that is on Sunday—"and Thomas was with them. Though the doors were locked, Jesus came and stood among them and said, 'Peace be with you' " (20:26, NIV).

This time when all Eleven were present, Jesus said to Thomas, "Reach hither thy finger, and behold my hands; and reach hither thy hand, and thrust it into my side: and be not faithless but believing" (v. 27).

The reaction of the Eleven. Did Thomas examine Jesus' wounds? John did not say. But he did write: "And Thomas answered and said unto him, My Lord and my God" (v.28).

* * *

The seventh appearance. At last we have an appearance in Galilee! This is another appearance that was only recorded by John. The background is fascinating; for at this time, Jesus had honored Peter by appearing to him on three separate occasions: (1) On his *third* appearance. (2) When he was with the Ten. This was the occasion when Jesus breathed on them and said, "Receive ye the Holy Ghost" (John 20:22). (3) When he was with the Eleven. But in spite of this, Peter's mind kept flashing back to the joys he had experienced on Lake Galilee.

John has provided an illuminating insight about this third occasion. "Simon Peter saith unto them, I go a a-fishing. They [Thomas, Nathaniel, James and John, and two other disciples] say unto him, We also go with thee. They went forth, entered into a ship immediately: and that night they caught nothing" (21:3).

Wearily, the tired and discouraged men glanced anxiously toward the rim of the lake. There, they noticed a man who'd been watching them. John explained: "Jesus stood on the shore: but the disciples knew not that it was Jesus" (v. 4).

"Children, have you any meat?" asked Jesus.

"No," they shouted.

"Throw your net on the right side of the boat and you will find some," replied the man they still did not recognize (v. 6, NIV).

Obeying the stranger's suggestion, the fishers threw the net onto the other side; and to their dismay it immediately filled with fish. Jaws sagging, the seven were dumbfounded. Then John said to Peter, "It is the Lord!"

Hearing that, Peter hurriedly flung an outer garment around himself to cover his nakedness, leaped into the water—and started for the shore. Those on the ship—it was only about one hundred yards from land—remained on deck while they towed the net behind them.

As they stepped onto the sand they discovered that Jesus had kindled a fire and that low flames were trembling just above a bed of glowing coals. They also noticed that he was broiling a "fish." The possibility that the word *fish* in verse nine was singular has been suggested by F. F. Bruce. "It is possible that thus far only one fish was broiling on the charcoal fire: the Greek singular *opsarion* might have this meaning or it might be collective like our word fish."

Heavy-muscled Peter then returned to the ship "and drew the net to land full of great fishes, an hundred and fifty and three" (v. 11).

Miraculously, even though he had to drag it over the sand in shallow water, the net was not damaged.

As the seven watched, they were overwhelmed by wonder, for by now they had all been completely convinced that the man by the fire was Jesus. "The disciples were [then] told," continued Bruce, "to bring some of their *opsaria* (plural). The noun *opsarion* is peculiar to this Gospel in the New Testament; it [had] been used earlier of the two fish which were multiplied in the feeding of the five thousand (John 6:9, 11)" (1983, 401).

When the fish were ready Jesus invited them to "come and dine"; and, as they surrounded the burning coals, he handed each a portion of bread and fish.

After they had eaten their breakfast, Jesus turned to Peter and began his oft-quoted conversation with him. This is how it is recorded in the NIV:

"Simon son of John, do you really love me more than these?"

"Yes, Lord," he said, you know I love you."

"Jesus said, "Feed my lambs."

"Again Jesus said, Simon son of John, do you really love me?"

He answered, "Yes, Lord, you know that I love you."
Jesus said, "Take care of my lambs."

The third time he said to him, "Simon son of John, do you love me?"

Peter was hurt because Jesus asked him the third time, "Do you love me?" He said, "Lord, you know all things, you know that I love you."

Jesus said, "Feed my lambs" (21:15).

The reaction of the Seven. After Jesus had told Peter for the third time "feed my sheep," he led the group in a leisurely stroll on the beach. Then as the smell of the fire and the lake and the fish drifted over to them, and as the fishermen felt the crunch of sand beneath their feet, Jesus faced Peter, and solemnly added: "I tell you the truth, when you were younger you dressed yourself and went where you wanted; but when you are old you will stretch out your hands, and someone will dress you and lead you where you do not want to go" (v. 18).

As Peter listened with frightened interest, he remembered how Jesus had been nailed to the cross; and he surmised that Jesus was now telling him that he would experience a similar fate. In the extreme silence that ensued, Jesus climaxed his statement with two solemn words the world can never forget: "Follow me!"

Shaken to the depths, Peter motioned toward John who was lingering nearby. "What about him?" he demanded.

Not wasting a syllable, Jesus answered: "If I want him to remain alive until I return, what is that to you?" (v. 22, NIV).

Those startling words remained with Peter and the others the rest of their lives. Each was inspired to keep preaching even though all of them with the exception of John died as martyrs.

* * *

The eighth appearance. This appearance—Matthew 28:16-20 and Mark 16:15-18—was to the Eleven on a mountain in Galilee where Jesus had instructed them to go. Mark tells us that when Jesus appeared to those who had followed him during his entire ministry "he rebuked them for their lack of faith and their stubborn refusal to believe those who had seen him after he had risen" (v. 14, NIV).

Then, amazingly, after having "rebuked them for their lack of faith," he hurled the great commission at them: "All authority in heaven and on earth has been given unto me. Therefore go and make disciples of all nations, baptizing them in the name of the Father and of the Son and of the Holy Spirit, and teaching them to obey everything I have commanded you. And surely I am with you always, to the very end of the age" (Matt. 28:18-20). See also Mark 16:15-18.

The reaction of the Eleven. Since both Matthew and Mark conclude abruptly at this point, it is reasonable to assume that the authors were convinced that their readers would understand that the Eleven obeyed Jesus and went into the entire known world and made disciples.

* * *

The ninth and tenth appearances. Since both these appearances are mentioned only by Paul (1 Cor. 15:6-7), some have identified them with the eighth appearance on the mountain. Others have even questioned their authenticity; for, at the time of the appearances, Paul had not yet been converted. His statement reads: "After that he was seen of above five hundred brethren at once; of whom the greater part remain unto this present, but some are fallen asleep. After that he has seen of James; then all the apostle" (vv. 6-7).

Can we believe that these appearances are separate from the others? G. Campbell Morgan's reply is "While we cannot be dogmatic, I think we have. He said to the women to tell his disciples to go into Galilee, where they should see him . . . I think as they went, the news spread, scores and hundreds, five hundred disciples of Jesus, perhaps frightened by the cross, gathered to him, and five hundred of them saw him" (Morgan 1946, 186).

Since Paul had undoubtedly personally met many of the five hundred, his statement has an extra ring of authenticity to it.

After this meeting Jesus appeared to James, and since

Paul mentioned this appearance right after that of his appearance to the Twelve and the five hundred, and then just before his final meeting with "all the apostles," we can be almost certain that this James was John's brother.

* * *

Can You Answer?

1. How many kinds of food did the resurrected Christ eat with the disciples and those who were on their way to Emmaus?
2. How did Jesus serve the bread?
3. What unusual effect did the eating of bread have on those who ate it?
4. How did Jesus prove to Thomas that he had a real body?
5. How often was Cleopas mentioned in the New Testament?
6. Were the ten disciples alone when Jesus appeared to them?
7. Peter's martyrdom was unique, but can you find in the Bible the name of the first martyred apostle?
8. How many wrote about Jesus' appearance to the five hundred?

11 Did Jesus Really Rise From the Dead?

In spite of New Testament documents, skeptics continue to insist that Jesus Christ was never resurrected from the dead.

A favorite argument tossed at believers is this: "If Jesus was actually resurrected from the dead, why did the writers wait scores of years before publishing such sensational news?" And another—a sneering one—demands why there are so many conflicts in the Gospels concerning the resurrection.

These questions demand answers.

Let's start with the first.

Why did Matthew, Mark, Luke, John, and Paul wait so long to record such exciting—and world-changing news? That is a formidable problem! Nonetheless, there are answers. One is that a week after Jesus' resurrection, his rising from the dead was no longer news—at least not in

Israel. Jesus having appeared to so many, the fact of his resurrection had been passed on to the entire nation by pilgrims who had been to the Passover.

Another facet that gleams like an oasis is that Jesus' resurrection was underlined with *urgency*. When Mary Magdalene discovered that the stone had been rolled from the tomb, the women immediately obeyed the angelic command. Using verbs, Mark exclaimed, "They *went* out *quickly*, and *fled* from the sepulchre, for they trembled and were amazed" (16:8, emphasis added).

How did Peter and John respond when breathless Mary Magdalene rushed over with the news? "They *ran* both together: and the other disciple did outrun Peter, and came first to the sepulchre" (John 20:4, emphasis added).

The urgency to report the resurrection originated with Jesus himself. While in his resurrected body, his final command was underlined with utmost exigency: "Go . . . baptize . . . teach all nations," and he added emphasis to his instructions by promising that he would be with them always, "to the very end of the age" (28:20, NIV).

Being witnesses to his power to heal, transform, and even raise the dead, and remembering Jesus' solemn words in the Upper Room: "He that believeth on me, the works that I do shall he do also; and greater works than these shall he do; because I go unto my Father" (14:12), the apostles burned with passion to proclaim to the entire world the transforming message that had been entrusted to them. With this news throbbing in their hearts, they could not be persuaded to waste a moment.

The words of Jesus were immortal; and yet, other than for a sentence in the sand, there is no record that he wrote anything. Nor did he request anyone to take notes on his sermons and parables. His thundering instructions to the apostles were GO! Moreover, they WENT!

Following their Holy Spirit baptism on the Day of Pentecost, the apostles were endued with so much power that they were accused of "turning the world upside down." This power led to an incident that confirmed beyond doubt that Jesus Christ, virgin-born Son of God, had emerged from the tomb on the third day after his death on the cross and was still alive.

* * *

In the third chapter of Acts, Luke recorded the remarkable story about how Peter and John went to the temple "at the hour of prayer, being the ninth hour"— the *very* hour Jesus provided atonement on the cross! At the "gate of the temple which is called Beautiful" they noticed a man who had been lame from birth and who was daily carried to this spot in order that he might beg.

Challenged by the opportunity to witness that Jesus Christ was not only alive, but remained with them, Peter and John "fastened" their eyes on the lame man. "Then Peter said: Silver and gold have I none; but such as I have give I thee: In the name of Jesus of Nazareth rise up and walk. And he took him by the right hand and lifted him up: and immediately his feet and ankle bones received strength. And he leaping up stood, and walked, and entered with them into the temple, walking, and leaping, and praising God" (3:8).

As the masses rushed to witness the reality of this miracle, Peter addressed them. His sermon was clear and yet diplomatic. After outlining the story of Jesus and how the mob had demanded the freedom of Barabbas and the crucifixion of Jesus, he added, "Now brothers, I know that you acted in ignorance, as did your leaders" (v. 17).

The fourth chapter of Acts informs us that as a result of Peter's sermon. about five thousand people were converted (v. 4).

Such success was too much for the authorities. Peter and John were jailed. Then they were taken to the Sanhedrin and stood before "Annas the high priest, and Caiaphas, and Alexander and as many as were of the kindred of the high priest" (v. 6).

When Peter and John were asked, "By what power, or by what name have ye done this?" (v. 7), Peter leaped to his feet.

As the Big Fisherman faced those who could demand his death, we wonder about the thoughts that may have sped through John's mind. Did he remember how Peter had denied that he knew the Lord to three different people on three different occasions? Did he remember Peter's blistering fishermen's oaths with which he intensified his outrageous, and incredible falsehoods?

Was he apprehensive about what Peter might say? He had reason to be concerned, for Annas and Caiaphas and their relatives glowered at Peter in an even more hardhearted way than they had glowered at Jesus during his trials and crucifixion.

The face of Caiaphas was brazen. His sullen eyes were more determined than ever. His lips—twisted like a snake prepared to strike—were ready to demand a double crucifixion.

But John need not have worried, for his friend was now dominated by the Holy Spirit. Erect before this gathering of leaders who detested him, he was as cool and confident as he had been when he made his great confession, "Thou art the Christ, the Son of the living God" (Matt. 16:16).

Facing Caiaphas and Annas and their henchmen, he said, "Rulers and elders of the people! If we are being called to account today for an act of kindness shown to

a cripple and are asked how he was healed, then know this, you and all the people of Israel: It is by the name of Jesus Christ of Nazareth, whom you crucified but whom God raised from the dead, that this man stands before you healed. He is
'the stone you builders rejected,
which has become the capstone' "
(Acts 4:8-11).

* * *

"Salvation is found in no one else, for there is no other name under heaven given to men by which we must be saved" (v. 12).

Shaken by Peter's courage and the power of his speech, and realizing that both he and John were uneducated and thus had a power from outside themselves, they released them with a warning that they were to speak no longer "to anyone in this name."

Why didn't Annas and Caiaphas deny the resurrection of Jesus? *For the simple reason that everyone in Jerusalem realized that his resurrection was a fact!*

Overwhelmed with the reality that Jesus was alive and that they had constant contact with him, the Eleven emphasized his resurrection wherever they went. That Jesus had conquered death was central in Peter's sermon on the Day of Pentecost and at his trial before the Sanhedrin. Thus, when they decided to replace Judas in order to restore their number to twelve, they decreed that no one could be one of their number unless he had been a witness with them "of [Jesus'] resurrection" (Acts 1:22).

* * *

At first, when the Twelve hurried from place to place relating the good news of Jesus Christ, the only book available to them was the Septuagint—the translation of the Old Testament into Koine Greek. Nonetheless, they had *memories!* And just as Jesus had promised in the Upper Room, "But the Comforter, which is the Holy Ghost, whom the Father will send in my name, he shall teach you all things, and bring all things to your remembrance, whatsoever I have said unto you" (John 14:26), they were comforted and empowered by him.

Driven by memories and motivated by the fact of the resurrection, their sermons were simple. Relying on the Septuagint they spread the news that Jesus was the Messiah about whom the prophets had written. Also they preached: *We knew him! We listened to him! We saw him die on a cross! We saw him after his resurrection! We ate with him! We saw his wounds! We witnessed his ascension! We speak to him daily!*

As they sailed the seas, the masts on the ships reminded them of the cross; as they trudged the Roman highways, the tombs housing the dead along the sides of the road inspired them by proclaiming loudly with silent voices that Jesus' tomb just outside Jerusalem was empty.

The world they lived in was a most difficult world. Augustus Caesar who ruled the Roman Empire at the time of Jesus' birth was a capable, and yet extremely wicked man. Murder meant nothing to him. Suffering from lameness and indigestion, he vented his wrath on anyone who got in his way. Augustus was followed by Tiberius, a pervert whose slobbering lips ordered so many deaths he was dubbed "Mud-and-Blood" and "The Old Goat." His rule from A.D. 14-37 crossed the ministry of both John the Baptist and Jesus. A Roman scrawled on a wall in a back alley the opinion of many in regard to this "Mama's Boy":

He is not thirsty for neat wine
As he was thirsty then,

But warms him up a tastier cup—
The blood of murdered men.

* * *

Tiberius was smothered by Caligula, nicknamed Little Boots. Now that he was Emporer, Caligula forced his own sister to divorce her husband and marry him. One of his hobbies was to order people to commit suicide. While sitting at a table with numerous guests, he burst into hilarious laughing.

"What's so funny?" ventured a guest.

"Oh, I was just thinking that with the mere nod of my head I could have all your throats cut!"

Little Boots declared that he was a god, and ordered the heads of the statues of the various gods removed and replaced with replicas of his own head.

Eventually, Caligula was murdered by his own bodyguard (Ludwig 1983, 28).

But as evil as the Romans were, they at first did little to hinder the advance of Christianity. To them, Christianity was just another Jewish sect that wasn't worth a shrug.

The main antagonists were Jews.

Just as the digit zero frightened merchants, Christianity frightened Judaism. That dreadful circle with nothing in it, which had been developed around 300 B.C., simplified things too much! "If, for instance, the Persians wished to express the number five million eleven thousand one hundred sixty-seven, they did it as 23, 11, 59, 27—which means $23 \times 60^3 + 11 \times 60^2 + 59 \times 60^1 + 27 \times 60^0$ (4,968,000 + 39,600 + 3,540 + 27 = 5,011,167)" (Bergamini 1963, 16).

Being able with the use of the digit zero to write five million, eleven thousand one hundred sixty-seven simply as 5,011,167 was too easy. Merchants were frightened because of the easy way it reduced the problems of multiplication and division. "By the late 13th century the city-state of Florence was passing laws against the use of the upstart decimal numerals to protect honest citizens from the easy changes which forgers of bank drafts, for instance, could ring on the numbers 0, 6 and 9" (17).

Used to the many rituals on the Day of Atonement, the Feasts of Passover and Unleavened Bread, the Feast of Weeks, the Feast of Purim, and numerous others, the rabbis were dismayed at the idea that a thief on a cross could have his sins forgiven and be promised immortality by just making a nine-word request.

To the Jews, the doctrine that a mere word with Christ could replace the tens of thousand of choice animals that crowded the streets on their way to be sacrificed, was blasphemy in its vilest and most shocking form. Years later, this blasphemy was darkened by the author of the Book of Hebrews.

After describing the old rituals in chapter nine, which included "the blood of goats and bulls and the ashes of a heifer" (v. 13), he pinpointed the fact the Jesus had provided a better way: "For this reason Christ is the mediator of a new covenant, that those who are called may receive the promised eternal inheritance—now that he has died as a ransom to set them free from the sins committed under the first covenant" (v. 15).

This declaration was like fire in the eyes of Judaism. Then Paul pushed the live coals into their eyes by explaining: "Wherefore the law was our schoolmaster to bring us unto Christ, that we might be justified by faith. But after that faith is come, we are no longer under a schoolmaster" (Gal. 3:24-25).

Confronted with the tidal wave of thousands accepting Christ, the apostles were herded to the Sanhedrin where they were questioned by Caiaphas. The high priest's accusation was a sizzling one: Luke recorded it in the fifth chapter of Acts: "We gave you strict orders not to teach in this name," he stormed. "Yet you have filled Jerusalem with your teaching and are determined to make us guilty of this man's blood" (v. 18).

"Peter and the other apostles replied: 'We must obey God rather than men! The God of our fathers raised Jesus from the dead—whom you had killed'" (vv. 29-30, NIV).

After Peter sat down, Gamaliel took the floor. Being a highly honored doctor of the law, the eyes of the assembly focused on him. The concluding statement of this respected Pharisee jolted them: "In the present case I advise you: Leave these men alone! Let them go! For if their purpose or activity is of human origin, it will fail. But if it is from God, you will not be able to stop these men; you will only find yourselves fighting against God" (vv. 38-39, NIV).

His speech persuaded them. Still, they had the apostles flogged, and then after ordering them not to speak in the name of Jesus, they released them.

Joyfully, Luke recorded, "The apostle left the Sanhedrin, rejoicing because they had been counted worthy of suffering disgrace for the Name. Day after day in the temple courts and from house to house, they never stopped teaching and proclaiming the good news that Jesus is the Christ" (v. 41, NIV).

Although not apostles, Mark and Luke kept just as busy as the Twelve. John Mark wrote the first Gospel— the one that bears his name. Mark had wide perspective of the life and death and resurrection of Jesus. He had labored with, and was then rejected by, Paul. Next, he stood side by side with Peter and interpreted for him. Besides his work in Africa, Mark labored in Turkey, Babylon, and other places. (See 1 Peter 5:13.)

After eleven years, John Mark was reconciled to the distinguished apostle to the Gentiles, and Paul gave testimony to this reconciliation. In his final epistle he wrote, "Only Luke is with me. Take Mark and bring him with thee: for he is profitable to me for the ministry" (2 Timothy 4:11).

While in Rome, "Mark the disciple of Peter, wrote a short gospel at the request of the brethren at Rome embodying what he had heard Peter tell. When Peter had heard this, he approved it and published to the churches to be read by his authority" (McBirnie 1974, 253-254).

Mark's "short gospel" was used extensively by both Matthew and Luke. An estimated ninety-six percent of Mark is found in one form or another in the other synoptic Gospels.

The Gospel of John was written many years later, perhaps as late as A.D. 95-100.

But are the Four Gospels Authentic?

Tireless scholars who have spent their lives studying the "synoptic problem" are, on the whole, agreed that they have recorded correctly the birth, message, passion—and resurrection of Jesus. The fact that there are numerous minor differences that have, so far, been impossible to harmonize, does not weaken them. The fact is, the differences strengthen their authenticity by showing that all four of the writers did *not* collaborate as conspirators to put something over on the public.

Numerous unadorned facts prove in their own mysterious ways that the Gospels were inspired by the Holy Spirit even though the Spirit used human beings to accomplish this purpose. Here are a few of those facts:

1. Blaise Pascal the supergenius who composed a *Geometry of Conics* at the age of sixteen and developed an adding machine, wrote: "The style of the Gospels is remarkable in many ways. One characteristic of them is that they never heap invective against the executioners and enemies of Christ" (Houston n.d., 201).

Having heard the crowds shouting "Crucify him! Crucify him!" how could the writers refrain from using strong language to describe them? *Because Jesus was alive, and was with them!*

* * *

2. "It is noteworthy that, while the four canonical Gospels could afford to be published anonymously, the apocryphal gospels which began to appear from the mid-second century onward claimed (falsely) to be written by apostles or other persons closely associated with the Lord" (Bruce 1983, 1). Why didn't Matthew, Mark, Luke, and John sign their names? Because they were writing what the Holy Spirit inspired them to write!

* * *

3. Also remarkable is the fact that the Gospel writers transcribed the truth without fearing that they might hurt someone. Mark had been Peter's secretary and interpreter. Nonetheless, he recorded in painful detail how Peter had denied the Lord (14:66-72). Likewise, when Matthew wrote the Gospel that bears his name, he had no fear of reflecting on Jesus when he inscribed the genealogy of Jesus' stepfather, Joseph. With dark ink, he boldly included in Joseph's family tree names that we would not want mentioned if they were in our family trees.

A grim example is Judah. He raped his own daughter Tamar; and by her became the father of Perez and Zerah. Perez became another cog in Joseph's genealogy, as did Rahab the harlot, and Bathsheba, the one with whom David sinned against the Lord and who later became the mother of Solomon (See Matthew 1:1-16).

Those scandalous names did not deter Matthew, for

he had determined to write the truth. Moreover, he wrote the truth! From Jesus' own lips and example, he knew that he had a way of using people who had sinned for the good of the Kingdom!

In like manner the writers recorded the paradoxes of Jesus even though they knew that some of them would be hard to understand.

What did Jesus mean when, after he had insisted that we love our neighbors, preached: "If any man come to me, and hate not his father, and mother, and wife, and children, and brethren, and sisters, yea, and his own life also, he cannot be my disciple?" (Luke 14:26).

* * *

4. Those who have experienced the love of Christ, are like the man who was born blind. When those who wished to expel him from the synagogue insisted that Jesus was a sinner, he replied: "Whether he be a sinner or no, I know not: one thing I know, that, whereas, I was blind, now I see" (John 9:25). Thus, every Christian knows that Jesus was resurrected from the tomb. He knows this is true because he is aware of his presence!

* * *

Can You Answer?

1. Give one reason why the Gospel writers delayed in writing their books?
2. Did the Gospel writers sign their names to their work?
3. Which Gospel was the first to be written?
4. Is there any overlapping in the Gospels?
5. What are the apocryphal Gospels?
6. Who fought the Christians the most, the Jews or the Romans?
7. Which was the last Gospel to be written?

12 The Empty Tomb

Most Christian scholars are convinced that the tomb in which Jesus lay was not in Jerusalem at all, but outside the city walls. This is so, for the Book of Hebrews is categorical: "Wherefore Jesus also, that he might sanctify the people with his own blood *suffered without the gate*" (13:12, emphasis added). John added "Now in the place where he was crucified there was a garden; and in the garden a new sepulchre, wherein was never man laid. There laid they Jesus because of the Jews' preparation day; for the sepulchre was nigh at hand" (19:41-42).

But even though millions agree that Jesus rose from the dead, there is a difference of opinion as to the exact location of the tomb from which he emerged. In our time two locations are claimed to be authentic. Each has ardent defenders.

In order to be certain that they have been to the right tomb, many tourists visit both places!

To solve the problem of which tomb is the factual one, we must learn the reasons each tomb was claimed to be *the* historic tomb, and to do that we must shuffle the calendar back to the second century A.D.

Horrified that the "Lord's Sepulcher" was in the hands of Muslims, Pope Urban II urged Christians to forget their local quarrels and to win the sepulcher back by force. With this inspiration and support, the First Crusade was launched in 1096. Those initial crusaders—the word is from the Latin *crux* that means cross—painted Christian emblems on their shields, kissed their wives, and started out.

By 1099 they captured Jerusalem, and Godfrey of Lorraine was made the city's ruler with the coveted title "Defender of the the Holy Sepulcher."

The tomb captured by the crusaders is now enshrined in the Church of the Holy Sepulcher in the northwestern section of the Old City. But the one known as the Garden or Gordon's Tomb, a little north of the Damascus Gate, is becoming exceedingly popular. The debate that rages over the genuineness of the two sites will never be settled; but it is an interesting debate.

Those who follow the arguments learn much about the history of Christianity.

* * *

Much of the Church of the Holy Sepulcher was built by the early crusaders. Attempting to be as accurate as possible, they built on the site selected by Macarius, Bishop of Jerusalem. Concerning his selection, there are spine-tingling details.

When Macarius was a delegate at the famous Council of Nicaea in 325 A.D., he confided to Emperor Constantine that he had discovered the actual location of the Tomb. Constantine's eyes widened. After investigating the bishop's report, he ordered him to build a place of prayer on the spot that would be "worthy of the most wonderful place in the world."

How Macarius located the place is anyone's guess, for at the time it was beneath a huge temple of Venus—the goddess of love! This fact is one that lends argument to the authenticity of the Church of the Holy Sepulcher. To understand this, we must retreat back to 135 A.D.

* * *

Roman Emperor Hadrian was a great traveler and a great builder. While in Britain in 122 A.D. he ordered the wall built from Tyne to Solway as a defence against the Picts and Scots. Ten years later he rushed his best general to Jerusalem to crush the revolt that had been launched by Bar Kokhba—an ingenious zealot who was accepted by many—including leading rabbis!—as the *real* messiah.

After Bar Kokhba's defeat, Hadrian completed the destruction of the city begun by Titus in A.D. 70. Having leveled and plowed it under, Hadrian ordered it rebuilt—in the manner of a Roman city. That was just the beginning of the insults he directed at the Jews.

The bearded emperor decreed that the figure of a pig should be carved over each gate in honor of the Tenth Legion, which had conquered the city under Titus, and that a temple to Jupiter be erected over the ruins of Solomon's Temple. He also insisted that a statue of himself be placed on the spot formerly occupied by the Holy of Holies.

Hadrian named the rebuilt city Aelia Capitolina. The Aelia glorified his own name: Publius Aelius Hadrianus. The Capitolina honored Capitoline Jupiter—the patron god of Rome.

Circumcised Jews were forbidden to enter the city,

and those who did were crucified. An exception was made each year on the ninth of Ab—the anniversary of the destruction of the temple. On that day, anyone could enter the city by paying a fee.

Christian Jews were never barred.

Having learned that a special hill was venerated by Christians, Hadrian decided to obliterate its memories forever. He attempted to do this by covering its most venerated areas with, as we have noted, the temple of Venus.

But instead of causing the site to be forgotten, the pagan temple marked the site for future generations; for it was a well-known fact that the Romans frequently tried to hide a shrine by building another shrine on top of it.

Eusebius wrote about the excavations that were removed from that venerated hill. "As one layer after another was laid bare, the place which was beneath the earth appeared; then forthwith, contrary to all expectations did the venerable and hallowed monument of our Saviour's resurrection became visible" (*The Empress Helena*, 28-30).

The crusaders did not consider Constantine's place of prayer at the "Tomb" to be adequate; and so they rebuilt and enlarged it. Today the area where the Tomb and the Cross were alleged to have been discovered, is filled with the liturgical equipment of the Roman Catholic Church. Lamps and candlesticks, yellow with gold, seem to be everywhere; and in their shimmering light one can see a steady stream of devout pilgrims flowing in and often passionately kissing what they consider to be a "sacred" spot.

Tens of millions are convinced that the Church of the Holy Sepulcher was built over the place where Jesus died and was resurrected from the dead. Likewise, tens of millions are convinced that the Church of the Holy

Sepulcher is not the correct place. These believers persist in reminding their opponents that Jesus "suffered and died without the gate," and the Church of the Holy Sepulcher is within the gates.

But that does not end the argument; for beneath the city are remnants of many walls; it is quite possible that a wall may have placed the Church of the Holy Sepulcher outside the gates.

* * *

On a trip to the Holy Land in 1958, I visited the Garden Tomb. After stepping through the gate, I was amazed when Dr. S. J. Mattar, the trim Arab keeper of the Tomb, invited me to stay for dinner.

As we waited for Mrs. Mattar to complete her preparations, Doctor Mattar showed me around the flowered and beautifully manicured grounds. Then he led me to the Tomb.

The Tomb is a rectangular cave carved out of rock on the low side of a rise known as Skull Hill. It came to the notice of General Chinese Gordon who was vacationing in Jerusalem after his campaigns in China. Observing a hill north of the Damascus Gate, he gradually became convinced that this might be the actual site of the crucifixion.

Later he noticed that there were two hollow spots, similar to eyes, on the rugged face of the yellow-tinged cliff. Using his imagination, he thought he could see the grim shape of a human skull. This increased his faith that this was indeed, the "place of a skull." But he faced a major difficulty, for John was specific in his description of the place where Jesus died: "Now in the place where he was crucified there was a garden; and in the garden a new sepulchre, wherein was never man yet laid (19:41). That passage meant that he would have to locate two things in the nearby vicinity: an ancient tomb and a place where a garden might have been.

The famous general went to work at once. Soon he found the tomb that had been discovered by the Greek. That tomb was only a few yards from the yellowing cliff with the hollow eyes.

Pulse racing, Gordon hurried to his New Testament to make comparisons. As he studied, his heart speeded. Everything seemed to fit! The place was *outside* the gate. It was within walking distance of Pilate's Hall. In addition, Gordon noticed that Mark had written: "There were also women looking on afar off" (15:40). This passage did not prove that the place of crucifixion was on a hill. But the words *afar off* suggested that it was at least on an elevated place that enabled the women to see over the crowd of taller men, and at a distance.

Gordon became so convinced that he had found the actual place of the crucifixion and resurrection drama that he drew sketches and dispatched them to Sir John Cowell, Controller of the Household at Buckingham Palace.

Soon interested Christians made an appeal through the *Times* for two thousand pounds with which to purchase the land containing the tomb.

That amount was raised, the land was secured, and in 1894 the *Garden Tomb Association* was formed in London. The place has been improved. There are now lovely walks, stone bridges, a house for the caretaker—and benches placed in strategic places. Many flowers mentioned in the Bible have been planted. There are low hedges of rosemary; brilliant patches of geraniums; tall, shady pines; and large areas of carefully mowed grass.

But is the Garden Tomb authentic? No one can be one hundred percent certain. However, several archaeologists have examined the Tomb and have agreed that it does goes back to the era of Herod the Great, the one who attempted to kill Jesus.

While the cistern was being repaired in 1952 workers discovered that the cistern, measuring fifty-six by thirty-three feet, was much larger than previously supposed—and, imbedded in Roman cement on a side of the wall, was a cross. That cross may indicate that the place had been used as a place of worship.

Could it be that some followers of Christ had chosen this place to worship because of the proximity of the Tomb? Perhaps!

A wine press has also been discovered within a few feet of the Tomb. This ancient press may indicate that the garden had belonged to such a wealthy person as Joseph of Arimathea. It also reminds one of the prophetic words of Isaiah: "I have trodden the winepress alone; and of the people there was none with me" (Isaiah 63:3).

* * *

As we viewed the Tomb and the Garden, Mrs. Mattar pointed to a table beneath some trees. "It's time to eat," she said.

The Mattars had six children, but since they were gone, just the three of us sat down before the delicious meal Mrs. Mattar had prepared. While we dined, Doctor Mattar told me that at one time he had worked in a bank at Haifa. In those days he owned considerable property, including a lovely farm in Cana of Galilee. When war broke out at the time of partition, he and his family fled to Jordan. Soon he was penniless. But God supplied his need in a miraculous way. Then he was invited to become the caretaker of the Garden Tomb.

During a lull in the conversation, I turned to Mrs. Mattar. "When did you become a Christian?" I asked.

"My mother, Lydia Nucho, showed me the Way."

"But how did your mother become a Christian?" I persisted.

"She heard an American by the name of H. M. Riggle preach under a tree in Nazareth. He baptized her in the Jordan River." That was stunning news, for H. M. Riggle was a popular American preacher I had known for years.

Alas, during the Six Day War of 1967, while hiding in the Tomb, Mattar stepped out to retrieve something from his home. At that moment, an Israeli soldier shot and killed him.

To millions, the Garden Tomb is the most renowned spot in the entire world.

* * *

Can You Answer?

1. Who was the "messiah" that was accepted by leading rabbis?
2. How did Hadrian attempt to obliterate areas considered sacred by Christians?
3. Who in the Christian era was first to destroy Jerusalem?
4. Who changed the name of Jerusalem to Aelia Capitolina?
5. Who was General Gordon?
6. What New Testament passages persuaded Gordon that the Garden Tomb was the authentic one?
7. Which keeper of the Tomb was slain during the Six Day War?

13 The Meaning of the Empty Tomb

Just as the digit zero revolutionized mathematics, the Empty Tomb has continuing potential to revolutionize lives. But since space is restricted, we must confine ourselves to the consideration of merely three of its life-changing powers.

In our society, anyone who has been physically wounded will attempt to hide the scars. (Cosmetics hide many of them.)

It was not that way with Jesus!

As jagged as his wounds were, he openly displayed them to the ten disciples (John 20:20). A week later he displayed them to the Eleven. Indeed, he not only displayed his wounds; but he also invited Thomas, "Reach hither thy finger, and behold my hands; and reach hither thy hand: and be not faithless, but believing" (John 20:27).

Overcome, Thomas exclaimed: "My Lord and my God!" (v. 28).

At first, the Eleven did not understand the meanings of this matter-of-fact display. They had seen Jesus heal the wounds of lepers. Why didn't he heal his own wounds?

But as they pondered they began to remember the words of John the Baptist who, when referring to Jesus, said: "Behold the *Lamb* of God, which taketh away the sin of the world" (John 1:29, emphasis added).

Impulsive Peter was perhaps the first to understand the real meaning of what John the Baptist had said. Like all Jews, he had sacrificed lambs to atone for his own sins; likewise, he remembered the ecstatic flush of forgiveness he had received when, after his denials, his eyes met the eyes of Jesus. That in-depth look had assured him that he had been forgiven.

Christ's atonement, and the depth of his atonement, have been demonstrated tens of millions of times. Indeed, the first reason for his death and resurrection was to redeem sinners.

* * *

Few crimes have stirred the public as much as the kidnapping and brutal murder of Bobby Franks by the two wealthy teen-agers Richard Loeb and Nathan Leopold, Jr. Defended by Clarence Darrow the trial dominated front pages around the world.

When the announcement was given that Darrow would begin his summation before Judge Caverly on August 22, 1924 in Chicago's Cook County Court Building, the courtroom was jammed to suffocation. It was so besieged that the bailiff's arm was broken. One woman fainted and had to be carried out.

A newspaper reported: "The crowd fought like animals."

Sixty-seven-year-old Darrow was completely prepared. Since the boys had pleaded guilty, his task was not to save them from imprisonment. Life imprisonment they could not escape. His task was to spare them from the gallows.

Employing every maneuver his brilliant mind could envision, he arranged for the boys to be tried before a judge rather than a jury. He knew that no judge would elect to shoulder the responsibility of personally sending two teen-agers to the gallows.

During his entire career Darrow relied on one system. He sought to persuade the judge and jury to be on his side, and then to show legal grounds on which to obtain the verdict he desired. Thumbs high in his suspenders, he hurled statistics, used sarcasm, quoted poetry. He appealed to the hearts of the scores of lawyers who had journeyed miles to hear him. He also appealed to the conscience of the judge:

> You may stand them up on the trap door of the scaffold, and choke them to death, but that will be infinitely more cold-blooded, whether justified or not, than any act that these boys have committed or can commit.
>
> I told Your Honor in the beginning that never had there had been a case in Chicago, where on a plea of guilty a boy under twenty-one had been sentenced to death. . . .
>
> Now Your Honor, I shall discuss that more in detail a little later, and I only say it now because my friend Mr. Savage—did you pick him for his name or ability or his learning?—because my friend Mr. Savage, in as cruel speech as he knew how to make, said to this court that we pleaded guilty because we were afraid to do anything else.

Throughout the trial, Darrow referred to Richard Loeb by his nickname Dickie and Nathan Leopold by his nickname Babe. Pressing home his reason for calling Nathan Babe, he remarked: "I shall call him Babe, not because I want to affect Your Honor, but because everybody else does. He is the youngest of the family and I suppose that is why he got his nickname." Then he added with a flick of sarcasm: "Mr. Crowe [State's Attorney] thinks it is easier to hang a man than a boy, and so I will call him a man if I can think of it."

Coatless, square-shouldered Darrow continued his summation in this manner for three days. The courtroom was like a furnace. But the listeners didn't mind. Occasionally mopping the few strands of hair that drooped over his eye, Darrow played his audience as a pianist plays the ivories.

As he sought to soften hearts, he repeatedly declared that in his opinion Dickie and Babe should remain in prison for the rest of their lives. Afraid that he had not yet saved them from the gallows, he thundered: "Your Honor stands between the past and the future. You may hang these boys; you may hang them by the neck until they are dead. But in doing it you will turn your face toward the past."

At about 4 P.M. on the third day his conclusion was personal: "I was reading last night of the aspiration of the old Perian poet, Omar Khayyám. It appeared to me as the highest that I can envision. I wish it was in my heart . . ." Voice quivering, amidst long silences as he vainly sought control, the Attorney for the Damned quoted Omar Khayyám's moving lines:

I do not care about that Book Above;
Erase my name or write it as you will,
So I be written in the Book of Love.

As he finished, tears were overflowing Judge Caverly's eyes. A newspaper reported: "The stuffed courtroom was like a black hole. Hardly a breath moved in it. Yet the crowd that was massed around Darrow sat motionless in attention as the weary old man gathered up all the threads of his argument for the final restatement."

Attorney Crowe took two days to sum up his conviction that the boys should be hanged. Nonetheless, the Old Lion had moved the judge and had provided legal grounds for life imprisonment.

Dickie and Babe were given life sentences.

* * *

We salute Darrow for unmatched court eloquence. Even so, the resurrected Christ does not argue our case in the manner of Clarence Darrow!

As "an advocate with the Father" (1 John 2:1), Jesus Christ does not plead for twelve hours, nor does he use sarcasm or speak of our youth or the way we've been affected by society—nor does he quote poetry.

His plea is similar to Darrow's at only two points: He admits our guilt; and he has thoroughly prepared our defense.

Although Darrow's lights burned late for months as he sifted evidence, thumbed shelves of musty law books, and interviewed psychiatrists and witnesses, his preparation could in no way be compared to the preparation Jesus Christ has made for our souls.

Jesus was with the Father from the beginning! He knew our histories before we were born! John reported him as saying "Before Abraham was, I am" (8:58). Thus we know that he understood our quirks, glands, and genes before we entered the world; and from the beginning, even before the fires in the sun were kindled, he prepared our defense—and spiritual healing.

How does he defend us? He pleads, Guilty on all counts! Then he makes a V with his arms, and murmurs,

I paid the price for sin. See the wounds in my hands, my feet, my side—and my head. These wounds are the receipts for the price I paid.

How does the Father respond? Guilty of both murder and adultery, David verbalized the cleansing he received: *"As far as the east is from the west, so far hath he removed our transgressions from us"* (Psalm 103:12). Furthermore, Jesus underlined the fact that David had been cleansed in the most dramatic way possible. While spikes tore at his hands and feet on the cross, he quoted David's opening to Psalm 22: "My God, why hast thou forsaken me?"

Unlike Omar's poem, one does not have to choose between the Book of Love and the Lamb's Book of Life; for after divine forgiveness, one's name is eligible for both books.

Thus a vital fact of the Empty Tomb states that because of the cross and the resurrection, anyone who pleads for pardon and accepts pardon will be completely forgiven of all the trespasses he or she may have committed.

* * *

A second attribute of the Empty Tomb is that we have the blood-edged promise: "I am with you always even unto the end of the world" (Matt. 28:20).

During the days of Jesus, a revered and yet despised name was Alexander the Great. Born in 356 B.C., Alexander was motivated by one flaming ambition. That burning ambition was to conquer the world and spread Greek culture everywhere.

Mounted on Bucephalus, twenty-two-year-old Alexander, along with his thirty thousand men, and five thousand cavalry, faced the vast, well-trained Persian army across the river Granicus.

Terrified because they were grossly outnumbered, an officer warned: "We'd better not attack today. This is June! June is an unlucky month."

Ignoring his advise, Alexander snapped: "Turn the calendar back. This is May, not June!" Alexander then plunged into the swirling stream and led his men to victory, even though the Persians had access to a million men.

The next year Alexander confronted six-hundred-thousand Persians on the plains of Issus. But even though they were led by King Darius III himself, Alexander defeated them. These victories were just the beginning. Cities and nations crumbled before his advance.

Alexander was an avid scholar and Homer's Illiad was his primary study-book. Indeed, the conqueror's copy had marginal notes by none other than Aristotle. And Alexander was determined to be the *new* Achilles.

At the head of his troops Alexander ventured out to conquer: Macedonia first and then India: up, over the lofty Himalayas and across the Indus to defeat King Porus.

By then, having been away from home for eleven years, his men were not interested in continuing on. In the manner of Achilles, Alexander retired to his tent and pouted. As he pouted he read the Illiad and poured over Aristotle's notes.

But now the Illiad and Aristotle's notes were as lifeless as sawdust. Finally, and with great reluctance, he headed for Macedonia. During his retreat, he tried to drown his sorrows with drink.

This prolonged drunkenness so weakened his body, he succumbed to a fever in Babylon. Like Jesus, he died when he was only thirty-three.

After their baptism with the Holy Spirit on the Day of Pentecost, the Twelve started out on their journeys to spread the Good News to the entire world.

Unlike Alexander, they did not have armies or a phalanx. Nor did they have a New Testament or a weekly check. But like Alexander they altered the calendar.

In honor of Jesus' resurrection on Sunday, they changed their day of worship from Saturday to Sunday. This change was revolutionary, especially to fellow Jews who had worshiped on Saturday for over a thousand years; but the apostles held firm, even though Sunday-worship brought down on their heads the wrath of the people. The first indication of this change was recorded by Luke: "Upon the first day of the week, when the disciples came together to break bread, Paul preached unto them, ready to depart on the morrow; and continued his speech until midnight" (Acts 20:7). See also 1 Corinthians 16:2, Revelation 1:10, and appendix for chapter 13.

* * *

Insistent tradition from many sources maintains that the Apostle Thomas went to India. In an interview with *Christian Life Magazine* (November 1954), Juhanon Mar Thomar, head of the Mar Thomar Church of South India, said: "According to tradition the history of the Mar Thomar Syrian Church goes back to the Apostle Thomas who landed, we are told, at Malabar, South India in A.D. 52 and founded several Christian churches. . . . Shut off by mountains on one side and the sea on the other, the Christians at Malabar lived, more or less, a life of isolation" (McBirnie 1974, 147).

As one thinks of the Apostle Thomas living in heat-drenched India, amidst non-Christian religions, and yet planting churches, one is faced with the question: How did he do it? The answer is: he was lead by the Holy Spirit, and he constantly remembered the words of Jesus: "Reach hither thy finger, and behold my hands; and reach hither thy hand, and thrust it into my side: and be not faithless, but believing" (John 20:27).

Unlike Alexander's Illiad, that memory never lost its power!

* * *

The power of the Holy Spirit and the resurrected Christ have continued to empower believers across the ages. When Polycarp was told either to offer a sacrifice to Caesar or be thrown to the wild beasts, he replied: "Eighty-six years have I served him, and he never did me any wrong. How can I blaspheme my King who saved me?"

Centuries after Polycarp, and a century before our time, the power of the Empty Tomb was still enabling believers to extend their reach. Following sixteen years in Africa, David Livingstone faced the greatest crisis of his life. In addition to the immediate peril, he had other troubles and heartbreaks.

Misunderstood by his board, he'd been forced to accept a position with the government. Also, he'd been stricken with illness. Acute diarrhea and repeated attacks of malaria had drained his strength for years. Likewise, vicious gossip had oozed through to him in regard to the character of his wife who was then with the children in England. But pushing these could-be tragedies from his mind, he wearily picked up his diary.

Supremely conscious of the resurrected Christ, he reached for his pen and wrote:

> <u>January 14, 1896. Evening.</u> Felt much turmoil of spirit in prospect of having all my plans for

the welfare of this great region knocked on the head by teaming savages tomorrow. But I read that Jesus said: 'All power is given unto Me in heaven and in earth. Go ye therefore, and teach all nations, and <u>lo I am with you alway, even unto the end of the world.</u>' It is the word of a gentleman of the most strict and sacred honor, so there's an end of it. I will not cross furtively tonight as I intended. Should such a man as I flee? Nay, verily, I shall take observations for latitude and longitude tonight, though they may be the last. I feel quite calm now, thank God!"

(All underlining was in Livingstone's own hand.)

But the power of the Empty Tomb is not confined just to the great. It is for everyone: the surgeon, the housewife, the factory worker, the preacher, the scientist, and the writer.

* * *

A third fact of the Empty Tomb is that it guarantees the teaching of Jesus that all believers will live again. Comforting Martha after her brother Lazarus died, Jesus was dogmatic. Said he, "I am the resurrection and the life. He who believes in me will live, even though he dies; and whoever lives and believes in me will never die" (John 11:25-26, NIV).

All Christians believe in the immortality of the human soul. Yet the bereaved are often faced with doubts and problems. After burying an old man whose life had been a success, Merton Rice hurried to the home of a couple whose baby had just died. He later wrote: I found a woman there who had . . . brought into the world [a] fragment of mortality that had breathed but a few hours. . . .

As we were coming back [from the cemetery],

the father said to me in a deeply searching way: "Mr. Rice, what is the use of having lived at all?"

It was a hard question.... That father was a mechanic and had dealt with mathematics enough to catch the meaning of a figure ... in calculus which looks like a figure eight lying sideways— ∞ . It means that any finite quantity in proportion to infinity gives the same result. . . .

He said he saw the reason for that. Then I said, "Let us now make a bit of human calculus with you, your babe, and you, or the old man from whose grave I have just come, or the oldest man who ever lived as the point of our reckoning. Grant me that the second of the human equation to be immortality, and then whatever you put on this mortal side of the sum, whether it be the eighty-four years of the last one I have buried or your own thirty years, or your babe's two days of life, the result is exactly the same; for, after all, the greatness of any human life is not how long it shall live on this earth, but rather that it is an immortal soul (Rice 1921, 15-17).

* * *

Face to face with the unlimited power of the Empty Tomb—the divine zero—what shall we do with this force that has removed the sting from death?

Students remember Thales of Miletus. This mathematician (640?-546 B.C.), discovered that "any angle inscribed in a semicircle is a right angle." Overwhelmed at his remarkable discovery, he sacrificed a bull in thanks to his gods.

Like Thales, should we make animal sacrifices or just

sit on a stump and look heavenward because of the divine zero instituted by Jesus? Neither! Jesus himself outlined our duties. We are to believe! Trust! Give! Obey! Forgive! Do! Receive!

* * *

Can You Answer?

1. Why didn't Jesus conceal his wounds?
2. In that Jesus is our advocate, how much time does he use when he pleads our cause?
3. What inspired Alexander the Great?
4. How long did it take for Jesus to prepare our plea?
5. What kind of comfort do we receive from the symbol used for infinity in calculus?
6. Who changed the day of worship from Saturday to Sunday?
7. Which apostle is believed to have evangelized South India?

Answers to Can You Answer?

Chapter 1

1. Jesus was nailed to the cross at approximately 9 A.M. Mark was categorical: "And it was the third hour" (15:25).

2. John's time differed from that of the synoptists because he wrote in Ephesis under a different system.

3. Since Jesus began his ministry when he was "about thirty" (Luke 3:23), was baptized in the "fifteenth year of the reign of Tiberius Caesar" (3:1), and his public ministry lasted approximately three years—John mentioned three Passover feasts—Jesus was about thirty-three at the time of his crucifixion.

4. Jesus' legs were not broken because he was already dead. (John 19:33). The Shroud of Turin confirms this (see Heller 1983, 83).

5. Three proofs that Jesus was really dead are as follows: (1) The soldiers did not break his legs; (2) A soldier pierced his side with a lance "and forthwith came there out blood and water" (John 19:34-35); (3) Joseph of Arimathea buried him (v. 38).

6. On which side of Jesus' body did the lance enter? Tradition insists that it was on the right side. Jim Bishop wrote: [The spear] "flipped forward and drove in between the fifth and sixth ribs. It went through the pleura and the thin part of the lung and stopped in the pericardium. The dead do not bleed, ordinarily, but the right auricle of the human heart holds liquid blood after death, and the outer sac holds a serum called hydropericardium. When the soldier withdrew the spear, blood and water were seen to emerge and drip down the side of the body" (see Bishop 1957, 309).

Also notice the comment of Doctor Pierre Barbet on page 13.

7. Pilate knew that Jesus was dead because of the report of the centurion he had sent to investigate. See Mark 15:44-45.

* * *

Chapter 2

1. The Koran (Qur'an) teaches that Jesus was born of a virgin. See *Islam* as edited by John Alden Williams (1962, 33).

2. The Koran insists that Jesus did not die on a cross—that the one who was crucified was merely "a likeness" (35).

3. Terry L. Miethe has explained that the word *grace* comes "From the Greek *charis*, 'graceful, agreeable." He defined it as "the gift of God, the unmerited favor of forgiveness or mercy given to sinners" (*Compact Dictionary of Doctrinal Words*).

4. An acrostic of *grace* is God's Redemption At Christ's Expense.

5. Grace is limitless. If a billion sinners sought grace at the same time, grace would not be diminished. "But where sin increased, grace increased all the more" (Romans 5:20, NIV).

6. Six reasons sustain the fact that it was Jesus who died on the cross and not a mere "likeness" as indicated in the Koran. (1) Jesus was led straight from Pilate's hall to Golgotha. (2) John, along with his mother and other women, watched him die. (3) While hanging on the cross, John along with his mother recognized his voice. (4) The sign, written by Pilate, was nailed onto the cross just above Jesus' head. It proclaimed boldly in three languages: JESUS OF NAZARETH THE KING OF THE JEWS. (5) Nicodemus, who knew Jesus well

helped bury him. (6). Those who passed by, together with the chief priests, scribes and elders, mocked him by saying "He saved others; himself he cannot save" (Matthew 27:39-43). The fact that these four groups recognized him, proves beyond doubt that he was the son of Mary, Jesus Christ of Nazareth.

7. Jesus was crucified on Friday, April 7, A.D. 29, at 9 A.M. (Mark 15:25). Notice chart in chapter 5, page 48.

8. Starting at noon the darkness lasted until 3 P.M., the ninth hour (Mark 15:33).

9. Jesus died at 3 P.M., the ninth hour (Mark 15:34).

* * *

Chapter 3

1. Joseph of Arimathea had to request the body of Jesus because Roman law required him to do so.

2. Jesus' last words on the cross were "It is finished" (John 19:30).

3. The darkness disappeared at 3 P.M., the ninth hour (Matt. 27:45).

4. The women went to the tomb as Jesus was being buried because they loved Jesus and perhaps because they wanted to make certain that Joseph and Nicodemus used sufficient spices.

5. The stone in front of the tomb was a wheel-size stone some six to eight feet in diameter and perhaps a foot thick.

6. If the Shroud of Turin is authentic, the linen cloth, had been woven in three-to-one herringbone twill.

7. Among numerous differences, the Pharisees believed in the resurrection from the dead while the Sadducees did not.

Chapter 4

1. A.U.C. means Ab Urbe Condita. Its first year was 753 B.C., the mythical founding date of the city of Rome; B.C. before Christ; A.D. Anno Domini; A.H. after Hegira—that is after Mohammed's escape to Mecca. Its first year was A.D. 622.

2. Second Adar, was the thirteenth month that was periodically inserted in the lunar Jewish year, in order to make the year have 365 days and stay even with the seasons.

3. The Caesars who ruled during the lifetime of Jesus were Augustus (31 B.C.-A.D 14), and Tiberius Caesar (14-42 A.D.).

4. Fish lacking scales (catfish, eels, and so forth) or fins (lobster, shrimp, octopus, and so forth) were forbidden. See Leviticus 11:12.

5. Jews generally only ate two meals a day.

6. A Sabbath day's journey was about three thousand feet.

7. Rabbis despised the Greek language, even though most educated Jews used it as a trade language.

8. The normal population of Jerusalem in the days of Jesus was approximately 150,000.

9. The Jewish Sabbath was on the seventh day—that is Saturday.

* * *

Chapter 5

1. Unlike our day, which starts at midnight and ends at midnight, the Jewish day started at sunset and ended at sunset.

2. Judas Iscariot was born in Kerioth—a city in the southern region of Judea. It may have been fortified.

3. Due to Dennis the Little's mistake, the Gregorian year in which Jesus was crucified was probably A.D. 29 or even earlier.

4. Judas did not betray Jesus for the money. It is quite likely that he betrayed Jesus in order to force him to set up an earthly kingdom in which the Romans would be pushed into the sea.

5. After the body of Jesus had been laid in the tomb, or maybe even before, he descended into paradise—hades—, for he had promised the thief: "Today shalt thou be with me in paradise" (Luke 23:43). But what is the meaning of hades?

Terry L. Miethe explained: "In the NT the term rarely appears. Jesus only used it four times (Matt. 11:23; 16:18; Luke 10:15; 16:23). In Luke 16:19-31, Jesus set forth the account of the rich man and Lazarus. Lazarus was in a conscious state and was being comforted. The rich man was also conscious, but he was in physical and mental torment" (*Compact Dictionary of Doctrinal Words* 1988).

This explanation is not the only one. Gleason's explanation on page 52 is the best I've seen.

6. Mary Magdalene was from Magdala now identified as Mejdel. This town, three miles from Capernaum, was renowned for its wealth—and immorality.

7. Tradition has it that Mary Magdalene was a prostitute; but this tradition cannot be proved by scripture.

8. Since Catholic dogma insists that Mary retained her virginity, they deny that she had additional children. But Matthew 13:55-56 not only lists four brothers: "James, and Joses, and Simon, and Judas," but also unnamed sisters. See Mark 6:3. Catholics maintain that these children were cousins.

9. Rabbis were required to see three stars before they blew their ram's horn to indicate the passing of the day.

* * *

Chapter 6

1. The word *passover* appeared for the first time in

Exodus 12:13. It indicated that the death-angel who had been instructed to "smite all the firstborn in the land of Egypt" (v. 12) would "pass over" those houses marked with the blood of the lamb.

2. The background for the Passover is in Exodus 21:1-51.

3. Jews have celebrated the Passover and still do, since the Exodus in the middle of the fifteenth century B.C.

4. Mary took Jesus to the temple when he was forty days old (Luke 2:22) in order to fulfill the law recorded in Leviticus 12:1-4.

5. Unleavened bread is prepared without yeast. It is eaten during Passover to commemorate the haste in which the Israelites fled Egypt (Deut. 16:3).

6. Sepulchers were whitewashed at Passover time because anyone who touched a dead body would be defiled and thus be excluded from the Passover Feast.

7. Passover was celebrated on the fourteenth of Nisan—late March or early April.

8. The foot-washing occasion in the Upper Room was only mentioned by John 13:4-14.

9. John did not mention the fact that Jesus instituted the Lord's Supper in the Upper Room.

* * *

Chapter 7
1. The new day was announced by the rabbis the moment the sun reached the western horizon.

2. Services in the temple were often changed across the centuries. Each change tended to make them more complicated.

3. There were always twelve loaves of unleavened showbread on display in the temple.

4. Showbread—Bread of the Presence—was made out of two tenths of an ephah—4 quarts—of extremely fine wheat flour.

5. The bread indicated that God provides our bread. The twelve loaves represented the twelve tribes of Israel.

6. On the First Sabbath of Passover, the initial psalm that was sung was the twenty-fourth which begins "The earth is the Lord's and the fullness thereof."

7. The scapegoat was to bear the sins of the nation and to atone for them by getting lost in the wilderness. See Leviticus 16:10.

8. The scapegoat was pushed over the cliff by a stranger.

* * *

Chapter 8

1. Jesus was "lost" in the temple at the age of twelve when his parents took him to the temple at the Feast of the Passover (Luke 2:45-49).

2. The women visited the tomb to express their love and to ascertain that the shroud was sufficiently spiced.

3. No one can be certain about the names of all the women who visited the tomb on Easter morning. Among them were Mary Magdalene, Mary the mother of James, the women from Galilee (Luke 23:55), Joanna—and, perhaps, Salome.

4. The women had no trouble finding the tomb for they'd been there before.

5. The fact that Matthew and Mark only referred to one angel does not mean that there was not another as mentioned by Luke.

6. John reached the tomb first.

7. John may have been the first to believe that Jesus had been resurrected.

Chapter 9

1. Having discovered that the stone had been rolled away during her *first* Sunday visit, Mary Magdalene returned to the tomb. It was on this *return* visit that she met Jesus.

2. Mary Magdalene did *not* recognize Jesus when he first appeared to her. Why? At first she was too startled. Also, he was in his resurrected body.

3. Why did Jesus instruct the women to inform the disciples that he would go before them into Galilee, and then appear to the ten in Jerusalem? Among the answers to this difficult question are the following: (A) when Jesus told the women to report to the disciples that he had risen from the dead, he may have had in mind his hundreds of disciples and not merely the Eleven. Informing those hundreds would take time; and thus his appearance to the Ten may have been a *preliminary* appearance; and (B) when Jesus gave the order to tell the disciples that he would meet them in Galilee, he did not mention a specific time; nor did he say that he would *first* meet them in Galilee.

4. Mary Magdalene was the first to inform Peter and John that the stone had been rolled away.

5. After introducing the Lord's Supper Jesus promised, "After that I am risen, I will go before you into Galilee" (Mark 14:28).

6. Peter and John ran to the tomb.

7. John remembered: "They ran both together: and the *other disciple* did outrun Peter, and came first to the sepulchre" (20:3, emphasis added). John, however, allowed Peter to enter first.

* * *

Chapter 10

1. After accompanying the two on their way to Em-

maus, Jesus stopped with them at one of their homes and ate bread. Later, while the two visited with the disciples in Jerusalem, he ate fish and a bit of honeycomb (Luke 24:42).

2. When Jesus served or ate bread, he "broke" it.

3. When Jesus supped with the disciples and the others in Jerusalem they were convinced that the man who appeared to them was *not* a ghost (v. 45).

4. Jesus proved to Thomas that he had a physical body by asking him to "Reach hither thy finger, and behold my hands; and reach hither thy hand, and thrust it into my side" (John 20:27).

5. Cleopas is only mentioned once in the New Testament (Luke 24:18).

6. The ten disciples were not alone when Jesus appeared to them. Those whom Jesus had accompanied on the way to Emmaus were present and so were those "that were with them" (v. 33).

7. The first apostle martyred was James the brother of John (Acts 12:2).

8. Jesus' eighth appearance, the one to the five hundred mentioned by Paul (1 Cor. 15:6), might have been the same appearance mentioned by Matthew (28:16-20) and Mark (16:14-16).

* * *

Chapter 11

1. The Gospel writers may have delayed writing the Gospels because they were busy proclaiming the good news. It could be they were nudged into finally writing them by the martyrdom of so many of their fellow apostles.

2. None of the Gospel writers mentioned their own names in their manuscripts. Still, there are solid reasons for believing that the names attached are correct.

3. Mark was the first Gospel to be written.

4. There is considerable overlapping in the Gospels. Approximately ninety-six percent of Mark is included with variations in the others. The first record of the Empty Tomb in the New Testament was written by Paul (1 Cor. 15:4-8). He may have seen a document describing the resurrection as early as his conversion in Damascus in approximately A.D. 34.

5. The apocryphal gospels were those that were not accepted by the early church. They were rejected because of their doubtful accuracy. Such apocryphal works include the Infancy Gospel of Thomas, the Prayer of Peter, the Book of Barnabas—and many others. Most are fanciful. For example: When the boy Jesus made clay birds, his birds flew!

6. At first, the Jews fought Christianity far more than the Romans.

7. The last Gospel written was John. It was written in Ephesus between A.D. 95-105.

* * *

Chapter 12

1. Simon Bar Kokhba (Son of a Star), led a revolt against the Romans from A.D. 132-135. Since he succeeded in throwing the Romans out, Akiba, a leading rabbi, announced that he was *the* fulfillment of Numbers 24:17—"There shall come a star out of Jacob." Eventually, Bar Kokhba was defeated. His followers then taunted his memory by sneering that his *real* name should be *Bar Coziba*—Son of Falsehood! (Ludwig 1983).

2. Hadrian attempted to obliterate areas Christians considered sacred by building pagan shrines over them.

3. Titus was the first Roman emperor in the Christian era to destroy Jerusalem. He destroyed it in A.D. 70.

4. After completely obliterating Jerusalem in A.D. 135, Hadrian had it rebuilt and renamed it Aelia Capitolina.

5. General Charles Gordon (1833-1885) was the distinguished British soldier who popularized the Garden Tomb. Famous for having captured Peking, he was dubbed Chinese Gordon.

6. The main New Testament passages that convinced Gordon the Garden Tomb was the authentic tomb were Mark 15:40; John 19:41; Matthew 27:33.

7. Dr. S. J. Mattar, the Arab keeper-of-the-tomb, was killed by an Israeli soldier during the Six-Day War.

* * *

Chapter 13

1. One reason Jesus exposed his wounds was to prove that he was the fulfillment of Isaiah 53:5 and similar passages.

2. Jesus takes just a moment to plead the cause of anyone who seeks his help. Jesus has never lost a case!

3. Alexander the Great was inspired by his copy of the Illiad, which had notations in it by Aristotle.

4. Jesus was preparing to plead our cause even before the beginning of time.

5. The symbol for infinity in calculus means that any number multiplied by infinity has the same result.

6. The day for Christian worship was changed from Saturday to Sunday in honor of the day of resurrection by the early Christians (Brown 1947, 257-262). Constantine merely legalized Sunday as the day set aside for Christian worship.

7. The Apostle Thomas has been credited with evangelizing India—especially South India. The many biblical names in South India lend weight to this tradition.

For Further Reading

The following additional books are among those I found to be especially useful.

Carnley, Peter. *The Structure of Resurrection Belief.* Oxford, 1987.

Edersheim, Alfred. *The Life and Times of Jesus the Messiah.* Hendrickson, 1986.

Eusebius, *Life of the Empress Helena.* n.d.

Footnotes for chapter 3:

1. A lentil is a small pea-like plant. Lentils are harvested and threshed in June. Red pottage is made by mixing them with flour. Sometimes the result is baked; at other times the mixture is served as a kind of porridge.

2. The Jews often sprinkled mint in their synagogues in order to produce a fresh smell. Likewise, it was served with meat dishes—especially with the roasted lamb during Passover. The Romans valued it for medicine, and Pliny reported that it was often mentioned in recipes.

Selected Bibliography

The following additional books are among those I found to be especially useful.

Carnley, Peter. *The Structure of Resurrection Belief.* Oxford, 1987.
Fuller, Reginald H. *The Formation of the Resurrection Narratives.* New York: Macmillan, 1971.
Gies, Miep. *Anne Frank Remembered.* New York: Simon and Schuster, 1987.
Kollek, Ted. *Jerusalem.* Weidenfield, 1968.
Kung, Hans. *Eternal Life.* New York: Doubleday, 1984.
Markxsen, Willi. *The Resurrection of Jesus of Nazareth.* Philadelphia: Fortress Press, 1970.
Miethe, Terry L. Did Jesus Rise from the Dead? The Resurrection Debate between Gary Habermas and Anthony Flew New York: Harper and Row, 1987.
Morgan, G. Campbell. *The Corinthian Letters of Paul.* Old Tappan, N.J.: Revell, 1946.
Morrison, Frank. *Who Moved the Stone.* Grand Rapids, Mich.: Zondervan.
Niebuhr, Richard. *Resurrection and Historical Reason.* New York: Scribners, 1957.
O'Collins, Gerald. *The Easter Jesus.* Dartman, Longman, & Todd, 1973.
Pascal, Blaise. *The Mind on Fire.* Houston James, ed. Portland, Ore: Multnomah Press, 1989.
Rosadi, Giovanni. *The Trial of Jesus.* New York: Dodd and Mead, 1905.
Seaver, George. *David Livingstone: His Life and Letters.* New York: Harper, 1957.
Stone, Irving. *Clarence Darrow for the Defense.* New York: Doubleday, 1941.
Weinburg, Arthur. *Attorney for the Dammed.* New York: Doubleday, 1941.

Works Cited

Archer, Gleason L. *Encyclopedia of Bible Difficulties.* Grand Rapids, Mich.: Zondervan, 1982.

Barbet, Pierre. *Doctor at Calvary.* New York: Doubleday, n.d.

Bergamini, David and the editors of Life. *Mathematics* Life Science Library. New York: Times Books, 1963.

Bishop, Jim. *The Day Christ Died.* New York: Harper and Row, 1957.

Brown, C. E. *The Apostolic Church.* Anderson, Ind.: Warner Press, 1947.

Bloch, Abraham P. *The Biblical and Historical Background of the Jewish Holy Days.* Ktav. 1978

Bruce, F. F. *The Gospel of John.* Grand Rapids, Mich.: Eerdmans, 1983.

Deedat, Ahmed. *Crucifixion or Cruci-fiction?* Durban R.S.A.: Islamic Propagation Centre, 1984.

Edersheim, Alfred. *The Temple, Its Ministry and Services.* Grand Rapids, Mich.: Eerdmans, 1950.

Frank, Anne. *Anne Frank: The Diary of a Young Girl.* New York: Doubleday, 1952.

Heller, John H. *Report on the Shroud of Turin.* Boston: Houghton Mifflin, 1983.

Josephus. *Antiquities of the Jews.* Book 20. Chapter 8.

Ludwig, Charles. *At the Cross.* Anderson, Ind.: Warner Press, 1989.

⸻ *Ludwig's Handbook of New Testament Rulers and Cities.* Denver: Accent Books, 1983.

McBirnie, William Steuart. *The Search for the Twelve Apostles.* Wheaton, Ill.: Tyndale House, 1974.

Miethe, Terry L., *Compact Dictionary of Doctrinal Words.* Minneapolis: Bethany, 1988.

Morgan, G. Campbell. *The Corinthians Letters of Paul.* Old Tappan, N.J.:, Revell, 1946.

Ribbentrop, Joachim von. *The Ribbentrop Memoirs.* Wiedenfeld and Nicholson, 1953.
Rice, M.S. *Dust and Destiny.* Nashville: Abingdon, 1921.
Rosadi, Giovanni. *The Trial of Jesus.* New York: Dodd and Mead, 1905.
Williams, John Alden, ed. Professor A. J. Arberry, trans. *Islam.* 1962.
Zarley, Kermit. *The Gospels Interwoven.* Wheaton, Ill.: Victor Books, 1987.